# TRAVEL
## THROUGH
# THE SOUTH OF
# FRANCE

# BY LIEUTENANT-
# COLONEL PINKNEY

FROM my earliest life I had most anxiously wished to visit France—a country which, in arts and science, and in eminent men, both of former ages and of the present times, stands in the foremost rank of civilized nations. What a man wishes anxiously, he seldom fails, at one period or other, to accomplish. An opportunity at length occurred—the situation of my private affairs, as well as of my public duties, admitted of my absence.

I embarked at Baltimore for Liverpool in the month of April, 1807. The vessel, which was a mere trader, and which had likewise some connexions at Calais, was to sail for Liverpool in the first instance, and thence, after the accomplishment of some private affairs, was to pass to Calais, and thence home. I do not profess to understand the business of merchants; but I must express my admiration at the ingenuity with which they defy and elude the laws of all countries. I suppose, however, that this is considered as perfectly consistent with mercantile honour. Every trader has a morality of his own; and without any intention of depreciating the mercantile class, so far I must be allowed to say, that the merchants are not very strict in their morality. Trade may improve the wealth of a nation, but it most certainly does not improve their morals.

The Captain with whom I sailed was a true character. Captain Eliab Jones, as he related his history to me, was the son of a very respectable clergyman in the West of England. His mother died when he was a boy about twelve years of age, leaving his father with a very large family. The father married again. Young Eliab either actually was, or fancifully believed himself to be, ill-treated by his step-mother. Under this real or imaginary suffering he eloped from his father's house; and making the best of his way for a sea-port, bound himself apprentice to the master of a coasting vessel. In this manner he continued to work, to use his own expressions, like a galley-slave for five years, when he obtained the situation of mate of an Indiaman. He progressively rose, till he happened unfortunately to quarrel with his Captain, which induced him to quit the service of the Company. In the course of his voyages to India, and in the Indian seas, he made what he thought an important discovery relative to the southern whale fishery: he communicated it to a mercantile house upon his return, and was employed by them in the speculation. He now, however, became unfortunate for the first time: his ship was wrecked off the island of Olaheite, and the crew and himself compelled to remain for two or three years on that barbarous but beautiful island.

Such is the outline of Captain Eliab's adventures, with the detail of which he amused me during our voyage. His character, however, deserves some mention. If there is an honest man under the canopy of Heaven, it was Captain Eliab; but his honesty was so plain and downright, so simple and unqualified, that I know not how to describe it than by the plain terms, that he was a strictly just and upright man. He had a sense of honour—a natural feeling of what was right—which seemed extraordinary, when compared with the irregular course of his life. Had he passed through every stage of education, had he been formed from his childhood to manhood under the anxious supervision of the most exemplary parents, he could not have been more strict. I most sincerely hope, that it will be hereafter my fortune to meet with this estimable man, and to enumerate him amongst my friends. I must conclude this brief character of him by one additional trait. A more pious Christian, but without presbyterianism, did not exist than Captain Eliab. He attributed all his good fortune to the blessing of Providence; and if any man was an example that virtue, even in this life, has its reward, it was Captain Eliab. In dangers common to many, he had repeatedly almost alone escaped.

I had no other companion but the worthy Captain: I was his only passenger, and we passed much of our time in the reading of his voyages, of which he had kept an ample journal. His education having been rude and imperfect, the style of his writing was more forcible than pure or correct. I thought his account so interesting, and in many points so important, that I endeavoured to persuade him to give it to the public; and to induce him to it, offered to assist him, during our voyage, in putting it into form. The worthy man accepted my offer, but I found that I had undertaken a work to which I was unequal. I laboured, however, incessantly, and before our arrival had completed so much of it, as to induce the Captain to put it into the hands of a bookseller, by whom, as I have since understood, it was transferred into the hands of a literary gentleman to complete. In some misfortune the manuscript has been lost; and the Captain being in America, there is probably an end of it for ever. All I can now say is, that the public have sustained an important loss.

In this employment our voyage, upon my part at least, passed unperceived, and I was at Liverpool, before I was well sensible that I had left America. Nothing is more tedious than a sea voyage, age, to those whose minds, are intent only upon their passage. In travelling by land, the mind is recreated by variety, and relieved by the novelty of the successive objects which pass before it; but in a voyage by sea, it is inconceivable how wearisome are the sameness and uniformity, which, day after day, meet the eye. When I could not otherwise occupy my mind, I endeavoured to force myself into a doze, that I might have a chance of a dream. One of the best rules of philosophy is, that happiness is an art—a science—a habit and quality of mind, which self-management may in a great degree command and procure. Experience has taught me that this is true. I had made many sea voyages before this, and therefore had repeated proofs of the observation of Lord Bacon, that, of all human progresses, nothing is so barren of all possibility of remark as a voyage by sea; nothing, therefore, is so irksome, to a mind of any vigour or activity. If a man, by long habit, has obtained the knack of retiring into himself—of putting all his faculties to perfect rest, and becoming like the mast of the vessel—a sea voyage may suit him; but to those who cannot sleep in an hammock eighteen hours out of the twenty-four, I would recommend any thing but travel by sea. Cato, as his Aphorisms inform us, never repented but of two things; and the one was, that he went a journey by sea when he might have gone it by land.

The sight of land, after a long voyage, is delightful in the extreme; and I experienced the truth of another remark, that it might be smelt as we approached, even when beyond our sight. I do not know to what to compare its peculiar odour, but the sensations very much resemble those which are excited by the freshness of the country, after leaving a thick-built and smoky city. The sea air is infinitely more sharp than the land air; and as you approach the land, and compare the two, you discover the greater humidity of the one. The sea air, however, has one most extraordinary quality—it removes a cough or cold almost instantaneously. The temperance, moreover, which it compels in those who cannot eat sea provisions, is very conducive to health.

We reached Liverpool without any accident; and as the Captain's business was of a nature which would necessarily detain him for some days, I availed myself of the opportunity, and visited the British metropolis. No city has been more improved within a short period than London. When I saw it before, which was in my earlier days, there were innumerable narrow streets, and miserable alleys, where there are now squares, or long and broad streets, reaching from one end of the town to the other: I observed this particularly, in the long street which extends from Charing Cross to the Parliament Houses. In England, both government and people concur in this improvement.

From London, finding I had sufficient time, I visited Canterbury, and thence Dover. If I were to fix in England, it should be in Canterbury. The country is rich and delightful; and the society, consisting chiefly of those attached to the cathedral church, and to such of their families as have fixed there, elegant, and well informed, I have heard, and I believe it, that Salisbury and Canterbury are the two most elegant towns, in this respect, in England, and that many wealthy foreigners have in consequence made them their residence.

Dover is an horrible place—a nest of fishermen and smugglers: a noble beach is hampered by rope-works, and all the filth attendant upon them. I never saw an excellent and beautiful natural situation so miserably spoilt.

The Captain being ready, and my necessary papers procured, I joined, and having set sail, we were alternately tossed and becalmed for nearly three weeks, and almost daily in sight of land. Some of the spring winds in the English seas are very violent. A favourable breeze at length sprung up, and we flew before the wind. "If this continues," said our Captain, "we shall reach Calais before daylight." This was at sunset; and we had been so driven to sea by a contrary wind on the preceding day, that neither the coast of England nor France were visible. From Dover to Calais the voyage is frequently made in four hours.

Several observations very forcibly struck me in the course of my passage, one of which I must be allowed to mention. I had repeatedly heard, and now knew from experience, the immense superiority of the English commerce over that of France and every nation in the world; but till I had made this voyage, I never had a sufficient conception of the degree of this superiority. I have no hesitation to say, that for one French vessel there were two hundred English. The English fleet has literally swept the seas of all the ships of their enemies; and a French ship is so rare, as to be noted in a journal across the Atlantic, as a kind of phenomenon. A curious question here suggests itself—Will the English Government be so enabled to avail themselves of this maritime superiority, as to counterweigh against the continental predominance of the French Emperor?—Can the Continent be reconquered at sea?—Will the French Emperor exchange the kingdoms of Europe for West India Colonies; or is he too well instructed in the actual worth of these Colonies, to purchase them at any price?—These questions are important, and an answer to them might illustrate the fate of Europe, and the probable termination of the war.

I must not omit one advice to travellers by sea. The biscuit in a long voyage becomes uneatable, and flower will not keep. I was advised by a friend, as a remedy against this inconvenience, to take a large store of what are called gingerbread nuts, made without yeast, and hotly spiced. I kept them close in a tin cannister, and carefully excluded the air. I found them most fully to answer the purpose: they were very little injured when I reached Liverpool, and, I believe, would have sustained no damage whatever, if I had as carefully excluded the air as at first.

## CHAP. II.
*Morning View of Port—Arrival and landing—A Day at Calais.—French Market, and Prices of Provisions.*

THE Master's prediction proved true, and indeed in a shorter time than he had expected. An unusual bustle on the deck awakened me about midnight; and as my anxious curiosity would not suffer me to remain in my hammock, I was shortly upon deck, and was told in answer to my inquiries, that a fine breeze had sprung up to the south-west, and that we should reach the port of our destination by day-break. This intelligence, added to the fineness of the night, which was still clear, would have induced me to remain above, but by a violent blow from one of the ropes, I was soon given to understand that it was prudent for me to retire. The crew and ship seemed each to partake of the bustle and agitation of each other; the masts bent, the timbers cracked, and ropes flew about in all directions.

It may be imagined, that though returning to my hammock, I did not return to my repose. I lay in all the restlessness of expectation till day-break, when the Captain summoned me upon deck by the grateful intelligence that we were entering the port of Calais. Hurrying upon deck, I beheld a spectacle which immediately dispelled all the uneasy sensations attendant upon a sleepless night. It was one of the finest mornings of the latter end of June; the sun had not risen, but the heavens were already painted with his ascending glories. I repeated in a kind of poetical rapture the inimitable metaphoric epithet of the Poet of Nature; an epithet preserved so faithfully, and therefore with so much genius, by his English translator, Pope. The rosy-fingered morn, indeed, appeared in all her plenitude of natural beauty; and the Sun, that he might not long lose the sight of his lovely spouse, followed her steps very shortly, and exhibited himself just surmounting the hills to the east of Calais.

The sea was unruffled, and we were sailing towards the pier with full sail, and a gentle morning breeze. The land and town, at first faint, became gradually more distinct and enlarged, till we at length saw the people on shore hurrying down to the pier, so as to be present at our anchoring and debarkation. The French in general are much earlier risers than either the Americans or the English; and by the time we were off the pier, about seven in the morning, half of the town of Calais were out to receive and welcome us. The French, moreover, as on every occasion of my intercourse with them I found them afterwards, appeared to me to be equally prominently different from all nations in another quality—a prompt and social nature, a natural benevolence, or habitual civility, which leads them instinctively, and not unfrequently impertinently, into acts of kindness and consideration. Let a stranger land at an English or an American port, and he is truly a stranger; his inquiries will scarcely obtain a civil answer; and any appearance of strangeness and embarrassment will only bring the boys at his heels. On the other hand, let him land in any French port, and almost every one who shall meet him will salute him with the complacency of hospitality; his inquiries, indeed, will not be answered, because the person of whom he shall make them, will accompany him to the inn, or other object of his question.

I have frequently heard, and still more frequently read, that the English nation were characteristically the most good-natured people in the world, and that the Americans, as descendants from the same stock, had not lost this virtue of the parent tree. I give no credit to the justice of this observation. Experience has convinced me, that neither the English nor the Americans deserve it as a national distinction. The French are, beyond all manner of doubt, the most good-humoured people on the surface of the earth; if we understand at least by the term *good-humour* those minor courtesies, those considerate kindnesses, those cursory attentions, which, though they cost little to the giver, are not the less valuable to the receiver; which soften the asperities of life, and by their frequent occurrence, and the constant necessity in which we stand of them, have an aggregate, if not an individual importance. The English, perhaps, as nationally possessing the more solid virtues, may be the best friends, and the most generous benefactors; but as friendship, in this more exalted acceptation of it, is rare, and beneficence almost miraculous, it is a serious question with me, which is the most useful being in society—the light good-humoured Frenchman, or the slow meditating Englishman?

There was the usual bustle, as to who should be the bearers of our luggage; a thousand ragged figures, more resembling scarecrows than human beings, seized them from the hands of each other, and we might have bid our property a last farewell perhaps, had it not been for the ill-humour of our Captain. He laid about him with more vigour than mercy, and in a manner which surprised me, either that he should venture, or that even the miserable objects before us should bear. Had he exerted his hands and his oar in a similar manner either in England or in America, he would have been compelled to vindicate his assumed superiority by his superior manhood. Here every one fled before him, and yielded him as much submission and obedience, as if he had been the prefect himself.

The French seem to have no idea of the art of pugilism, and with the sole exception of the military, no point of honour which renders them impatient under any merited personal castigation. They take a blow with great *sang froid*. Whether from good humour, or cowardice; whether that they thought they deserved it, or that they feared to resent it, the single arm of our Captain chastised a whole rabble of them, and they made a lane for as many of us as chose to land, accompanied by such porters as we had ourselves selected. Three or four of them, however, were still importuning us to permit them to show us to an inn; but as we had already made our selection in this point likewise, our Captain returned them no answer, but by a rough mimickry of their address and gesticulation.

After our luggage had undergone the customary examination by the officers of the customs, in the execution of which office a liberal fee procured us much civility, we were informed that it was necessary to present ourselves before the Commissary, for that so many Englishmen had obtained admission as Americans, that the French government had found it necessary to have recourse to an unusual strictness, and that the Commissary had it in orders not to suffer any one to proceed till after the most rigid inquiry into his passport and business.

Accordingly, having seen our luggage into a wheel-barrow, which the Captain insisted should accompany us, we waited upon the Commissary, but were not fortunate enough to find him at his office. A little dirty boy informed us, that Mons. Mangouit had gone out to visit a neighbour, but that if we would wait till twelve o'clock (it was now about nine), we should infallibly see him, and have our business duly dispatched. The office in which we were to wait for this Mons. Mangouit for three hours, was about five feet in length by three in width, very dirty, without a chair, and in every respect resembling a cobler's stall in one of the most obscure streets of London. Mons. Commissary's inkstand was a coffee-cup without an handle, and his book of entries a quire of dirty writing-paper. This did not give us much idea either of the personal consequence of Mons. Mangouit, or of the grandeur of the Republic.

The boy was sent out to summon his master, as a preferable way to our waiting till twelve o'clock. Monsieur at length made his appearance; a little, mean-looking man, with a very dirty shirt, a well-powdered head, a smirking, bowing coxcomb. He informed us with

4

many apologies, unnecessary at least in a public officer, that he was under the necessity of doing his duty; that his duty was to examine us according to some queries transmitted to him; but that we appeared gentlemen, true Americans, and not English spies.

After a long harangue, in which the little gentleman appeared very much pleased with himself, he concluded by demanding our passport, upon sight of which he declared himself satisfied, and promised to make us out others for passing into the interior. We were desired to call for these in the evening, or he would himself do us the honour to wait upon us with them at our hotel. Considering the latter as a kind of self-invitation to dine with us, we mentioned our dinner hour, and other *et ceteras*. Mons. Mangouit smiled his acquiescence, and we left him, in the hopes that he would at least change his linen.

Upon leaving the Commissary, our wheel-barrow was again put in motion, and accompanied us to Dessein's. This hotel still maintains its reputation and its name. After seeing almost all France, we had no hesitation in pronouncing it to be the only inn which could enter into any reasonable comparison with any of the respectable taverns either of England or America. In no country but in America and England, have they any idea of that first of comforts to the wearied traveller, a clean and housewife-like bed. I speak from woeful experience, when I advise every traveller to consider a pair of sheets and a counterpane as necessary a part of his luggage as a change of shirts. He will travel but few miles from Calais, before he will understand the necessity of this admonition.

We ordered an early dinner, and sallied forth to see the town. It has nothing, however, to distinguish it from other provincial towns, or rather sea-ports, of the second order. It has been compared to Dover, but I think rather resembles Folkstone. The streets are irregular, the houses old and lofty, and the pavement the most execrable that can be imagined. There was certainly more bustle and activity than is usual in an English or in an American town of the same rank; and this appeared to us the more surprising, as we could see no object for all this hurry and loquacity. To judge by appearance, the people of Calais had no other more important business than to make their remarks upon us as we passed their doors or shops. There was no shipping in the harbour, and even the stock in the shops had every appearance of having remained long, and having to remain longer in its fixed repose.

Being the market-day, we had the curiosity to inquire the price of several articles of provision, and to compare them with those of their neighbours on the opposite side of the channel. The market was well stocked; there was an incredible quantity of poultry, lamb, butter, eggs, and herbs. A couple of fowls were three livres, at a time that they were seven or eight shillings in London; a young goose, two livres twelve sous (2s. 2d.). Lamb was sold as in England, by the quarter or side, and was about sixpence English money per pound; beef about fourpence halfpenny, and mutton (not very good) fourpence. Upon the whole, the money price of every thing appeared about one-half cheaper than in England; but whether this difference is not in some degree compensated in England by the superiority of quality, is what I cannot exactly decide. The beef was certainly not so good as that to which I had been accustomed in London; but, on the other hand, in the progress of my journey, the mutton and lamb, when I could get it dressed to my wishes, appeared sweeter. The short feed gives it the taste of Welsh mutton, but the consumption of it is scarcely sufficient to encourage the feeders. The manner, moreover, in which these meats are employed and served in French cooking, is such as not to encourage the feeder to any superior care. Lean meat answers the purposes of *bouillé* as well as the fat meat, and it is of little concern what that joint is which is only to be boiled down to its very fibres. The old proverb, that God sent meats, and the d——l cooks, is verified in every kitchen in France.

We returned to Quillac's to dinner, which, according to our orders, was composed in the English style, except a French dish or two for Mons. Mangouit. This gentleman now appeared altogether as full-dressed as he had before been in full dishabille. We exchanged much conversation on Calais and England, and a word or two respecting the French Emperor. He appeared much better informed than we had previously concluded from his coxcomical exterior. He seemed indeed quite another man.

He accompanied us after dinner to the comedy: the theatre is within the circuit of the inn. The performers were not intolerable, and the piece, which was what they call a proverb (a fable constructed so as to give a ludicrous verification or contradiction to an old saying), was amusing. I thought I had some obscure recollection of a face amongst the female performers, and learned afterwards, that it was one of the maids of the inn; a lively brisk girl, and a volunteer, from her love of the drama. In this period of war between England and France, Calais has not the honour of a dramatic corps to herself, but occasionally participates in one belonging to the district.

The play being over very early, we finished the evening in our own style, a proceeding we had cause to repent the following day, as the *Cote rolie* did not agree with us so well as old Port. I suffered so much from the consequent relaxation, that I never repeated the occasion. It produced still another effect; it removed my previous admiration of French sobriety. There is little merit, I should think, in abstaining from such a constant use of medicine.

## CHAP. III.

*Purchase of a Norman Horse—Visit in the Country—Family of*
*a French Gentleman—Elegance of French domestic Economy—Dance*
*on the Green—Return to Calais.*

NOTWITHSTANDING the merited reprobation to be met with in every traveller, of French beds and French chamberlains, we had no cause to complain of our accommodation in this respect at Dessein's. This house, though it has changed masters, is conducted as well as formerly, and there was nothing in it, which could have made the most determined lover of ease repent his having crossed the Channel.

After our breakfast on the morning following our arrival, I began to consider with myself on the most suitable way of executing my purpose—of seeing France and Frenchmen, the scenery and manners, to the best advantage. I called in my landlord to my consultation; and having explained my peculiar views, was advised by him to purchase a Norman horse, one of which he happened to have in his stables; a circumstance which perhaps suggested the advice. Be this as it may, I adopted his recommendation, and I had no cause to repent it. The bargain was struck upon the spot; and for twenty-seven Louis I became master of a horse, upon whom, taking into the computation crossroads and occasional deviations, I performed a journey not less than two thousand miles; and in the whole of this course, without a stumble sufficient to shake me from my seat. The Norman horses are low and thick, and like all of this make, very steady, sure, and strong. They will make a stage of thirty miles without a bait, and will eat the coarsest food. From some indications of former habits about my own horse, I was several times led to conclude, that he had been more accustomed to feed about the lanes, and live on his wits, as it were, than in any settled habitation, either meadow or stable. I never had a brute companion to which I took a greater fancy.

Having a letter to a gentleman resident about two miles from Calais, I had occasion to inquire the way of a very pretty peasant girl whom I overtook on the road, just above the town. The way was by a path over the fields: the young peasant was going to some house a mile or two beyond the object of my destination, and, as I have reason to believe, not exactly in the same line. Finding me a stranger, however, she accompanied me, without hesitation, up a narrow cross-road, that she might put me into the foot-path; and when we had come to it, finding some difficulty in giving intelligibly a complex direction, she concluded by saying she would go that way herself. I was too pleased with my companion to decline her civility. I learned in the course of my walk that she was the daughter of a small farmer: the farm was small indeed, being about half an arpent, or acre. She had been to Calais to take some butter, and had the same journey three mornings in the week. Her father had one cow of his own, and rented two others, for each of which he paid a Louis annually. The two latter fed by the road-sides. Her father earned twenty sols a day as a labourer, and had a small pension from the Government, as a veteran and wounded soldier. Upon this little they seemed, according to her answers, to live very comfortably, not to say substantially. Poultry, chestnuts, milk, and dried fruit, formed their daily support. "We never buy meat," said she, "because we can raise more poultry than we can sell."

The country around Calais has so exact a resemblance to that of the opposite coast, as to appear almost a counterpart, and as if the sea had worked itself a channel, and thus divided a broad and lofty hill. It is not, however, quite so barren and cheerless as in the immediate precincts of Dover. Vegetation, what there was of it, seemed stronger, and trees grow nearer to the cliffs. There were likewise many flowers which I had never seen about Dover and the Kentish coast. But on the whole, the country was so similar that I in vain looked around me for something to note.

The gentleman to whom I had brought a letter of introduction was at Paris; but I saw his son, to whom I was therefore compelled to introduce myself. The young man lamented much that his father was from home, and that he could not receive me in a manner which was suitable to a gentleman of my appearance; the friend of Mr. Pinckney, who was the beloved friend of his father. All these things are matter of course to all Frenchmen, who are never at a loss for civility and terms of endearment. A young English gentleman of the same age with this youth (about nineteen), would either have affronted you by his sulky reserve, or compelled you as a matter of charity to leave him, to release him from blushing and stammering. On the other hand, young Tantuis and myself were intimates in the moment after our first introduction.

Upon entering the house, and a parlour opening upon a lawn in the back part, I was introduced to Mademoiselle his sister, a beautiful girl, a year, or perhaps more, younger than her brother. She rose from an English piano as I entered, whilst her brother introduced me with a preamble, which he rolled off his tongue in a moment. A refreshment of fruit, capillaire, and a sweet wine, of which I knew not the name, was shortly placed before me, and the young people conversed with me about England and Calais, and whatever I told them of my own concerns, with as much ease and apparent interest, as if we had been born and lived in the same village.

Mademoiselle informed me, that the people in Calais had no character at all; that they were fishermen and smugglers, which last business they carried on in war as well as in peace, and had no reputation either for honesty or industry; that she had no visiting society at Calais, and never went to the town but on household business; that the price of every thing had doubled within four years, but that the late plenty, and the successes of the Emperor, were bringing every thing to their former standard; that her father payed very moderate taxes; her brother stated about five Louis annually; but they differed in this point. The house was of that size and order, which in England would have paid at least thirty pounds, and added to this was a domain of between sixty and seventy arpents.

The dinner, whether in compliment to me, or that things have now all taken this turn in France, was in substance so completely English, and served up in a manner so English, as almost to call forth an exclamation of surprise. When we enter a new country, we so fully expect to find every thing new, as to be surprised at almost any necessary coincidence. This characteristic difference is very rapidly wearing off in every kingdom in Europe. A couple of fowls, a rice-pudding, and a small chine, composed our dinner. It was served in a pretty kind of china, and with silver forks. The cloth was removed as in England, and the table covered with dried fruits, confectionary, and coffee; a tall silver epergne supporting small bottles of capillaire, and sweetmeats in cut glass. The fruits were in plates very tastily painted in landscape by Mademoiselle; and at the top and bottom of the table was a silver image of Vertumnus and Pomona, of the same height with the epergne in the centre. The covering of the table was a fine deep green cloth, spotted with the simple flower called the double daisy.

I am the more particular in this description, as the dinner was thus served, and the table thus appointed, without any apparent preparation, as if it was all in their due and daily course. Indeed, I have had occasion frequently to observe, that the French ladies infinitely excel those of every other nation in these minor elegancies; in a cheap and tasteful simplicity, and in giving a value to indifferent things by a manner peculiar to themselves. Mademoiselle left us after the first cup of coffee, saying, that she had heard that it was a custom in England, that gentlemen should have their own conversation after dinner. I endeavoured to turn off a compliment in the French style upon this observation, but felt extremely awkward, upon foundering in the middle of it, for want of more familiar acquaintance with the language. Monsieur, her brother, perceived my embarrassment, and becoming my interpreter, helped me out of it with much good-humour, and with some dexterity. I resolved, however, another time, never to tilt with a French lady in compliment.

Being alone with the young man, I made some inquiries upon subjects upon which I wanted information, and found him at once communicative and intelligent. The agriculture of the country about Calais appears to be wretched. The soil is in general very good, except where the substratum of chalk, or marle, rises too near the surface, which is the case immediately on the cliffs. The course of the crops is bad indeed—fallow, rye, oats. In some land it is fallow, wheat, and barley. In no farm, however, is the fallow laid aside; it is considered as indispensable for wheat, and on poor lands for rye. The produce, reduced to English Winchester measure, is about nineteen bushels of wheat, and twenty-three or twenty-four of barley. Besides the fallow, they manure for wheat. The manure in the immediate vicinity of Calais is the dung of the stable-keepers and the filth of that town. The rent of the land around Calais, within the daily market of the town, is as high as sixty livres; but beyond the circuit of the town, is about twenty livres (sixteen shillings). Since the settlement of the Government, the price of land has risen; twenty Louis an acre is now the average price in the purchase of a large farm. There are no tithes, but a small rate for the officiating minister. Labourers earn thirty sous per day (about fifteen-pence English), and women, in picking stones, &c. half that sum. Rents, since the Revolution, are all in money; but there are some instances of personal service, and which are held to be legal even under the present state of things, provided they relate to husbandry, and not to any servitude or attendance upon the person of the landlord. Upon the whole, I found that the Revolution had much improved the condition of the farmers, having relieved them from feudal tenures and lay-tithes. On the other hand, some of the proprietors, even in the neighbourhood of Calais, had lost nearly the whole of the rents, under the interpretation of the law respecting what were to be considered as feudal impositions. The Commissioners acting under these laws had determined all old rents to come under this description, and had thus rendered the tenants under lease proprietors of the lands.

The young lady who had left as returned towards evening, and by her heightened colour, and a small parcel in her hand, appeared to have walked some distance. Her brother, doubtless from a sympathetic nature, guessed in an instant the object of her walk. "You have been to Calais," said he. "Yes," replied she, with the lovely smile of kindness; "I thought that Monsieur would like some tea after the manner of his countrymen, and having only coffee in the house, I walked to Calais to procure some." I again felt the want of French loquacity and readiness. My heart was more eloquent than my tongue. I rose, and involuntarily took and pressed the hand of the sweet girl. Who will now say that the French are not characteristically a good-humoured people, and that a lovely French girl is not an angel? I thought so at the time, and though my heart has now cooled, I think so still. I feel even no common inclination to, describe this young French beauty, but that I will not do her the injustice to copy off an image which remains more faithfully and warmly imprinted on my memory.

The house, as I have mentioned, opened behind on a lawn, with which the drawing-room was even, so that its doors and windows opened immediately upon it. This lawn could not be less than four or five English acres in extent, and was girded entirely around by a circle of lofty trees from within, and an ancient sea-stone wall, very thick and high, from without. The trunks of the trees and the wall were hid by a thick copse or shrubbery of laurels, myrtles, cedars, and other similar shrubs, so as to render the enclosed lawn the most beautiful and sequestered spot I had ever seen. On the further extremity from the house was an avenue from the lawn to the garden, which was likewise spacious, and surrounded by a continuation of the same wall. In the further corner of the latter was a summer-house, erected on the top of the wall, so as to look over it on the fields and the distant sea.

Tea was here served up to us in a manner neither French nor English, but partaking of both. Plates of cold chicken, slices of chine, cakes, sweetmeats, and the whitest bread, composed a kind of mixed repast, between the English tea and the French supper. The good-humour and vivacity of my young friends, and the prospect from the windows, which was as extensive as beautiful, rendered it a refreshment peculiarly cheering to the spirits of a traveller.

Before the conclusion of it, I had another specimen of French manners and French benevolence. A party of young ladies were announced as visitors, and followed immediately the servant who conducted them. Speaking all at once, they informed Mademoiselle T——, that they had learned the arrival of her English friend (so they did me the honour to call me), and knowing her father was at Paris, had hurried off to assist her in giving Monsieur a due welcome. They mentioned several other names, which were coming with the same friendly purpose; a piece of information, which caused the young Monsieur T—— to make me a hasty bow, and leave me with the ladies. He returned in a short time, and the sound of fiddles tuning below on the lawn, rendered any explanation unnecessary. We immediately descended; the promised ladies, and their partners, soon made their appearance; and the merry dance on the green began. As the stranger of the company, I had of course the honour of leading Mademoiselle T——. In the course of the dance other visitors appeared, who formed themselves into cotillions and reels; and the lawn being at length well filled, the evening delightful, and the moon risen in all her full glory, the whole formed a scene truly picturesque.

After an evening, or rather a night, thus protracted to a late hour, I returned to Calais; and was accompanied to the immediate adjacency by one of the parties, consisting of two ladies and a gentleman. I was assailed by many kind importunities to repeat my visit; but as I intended to leave Calais on the morrow, I made my best possible excuses.

## CHAP. IV.

*French Cottages.—Ludicrous exhibition.—French Travellers—Chaise de Poste.—Posting in France.—Departure from Calais.—Beautiful Vicinity of Boulogne.*

TWO days were amply sufficient to see all that Calais has to exhibit. After the first novelty is over, no place can please, except either by its intrinsic beauty, or the happy effect of habit. Calais, has no such intrinsic charms, and I was not disposed to try the result of the latter. I accordingly resolved to proceed on my road; but as the heat was excessive, deferred it till the evening.

The exercise of the preceding night had produced an unpleasant ferment in my blood, attended by an external feeling of feverish heat, and checked perspiration. Every traveller should be, in a degree, his own physician. I had recourse to a dip in the sea, and found immediate relief. Nothing, indeed, is so instantaneous a remedy, either for violent fatigue, or any of the other effects following unusual exercise, as this simple specific. After a ride of sixty or seventy miles through the most dusty roads, and under the hottest sun of a southern Midsummer, I have been restored to my morning freshness by the cold bath.

By the buildings which I observed to be going forward, I was led to a conclusion that Calais is a flourishing town; but I confess I saw no means to which I could attribute this prosperity. There was no appearance of commerce, and very little of industry. One circumstance was truly unaccountable to me. Though there were two or three ships laying unrigged, but otherwise sound, and in the best navigable condition, there was a building-yard, in which two new vessels were on the stock. These vessels, indeed, were of no considerable tonnage; but I confess myself at a loss to guess their object.

About a mile from Calais, is a beautiful avenue of the finest walnut and chestnut trees I have ever seen in France. They stand upon common land, and, of course, are public property. In the proper season of the year, the people of Calais repair hither for their evening dance; and such is the force of custom, the fruit remains untouched, and reserved for these occasions. Every one then takes what he pleases, but carries nothing home beyond what may suffice for his consumption on the way.

In my walk thither I passed several cottages, and entered some. The inhabitants seemed happy, and to possess some substantial comforts. The greater part of these cottages had a walnut or chestnut tree before them, around which was a rustic seat, and which, as overshadowed by the broad branches and luxuriant foliage, composed a very pleasing image. The manner in which the sod was partially worn under most of them, explained their nightly purpose; or if there could yet be any doubt, the flute and fiddle, pendant in almost every house, spoke a still more intelligible language.

I entered no house so poor, and met with no inhabitant so inhospitable, as not to receive the offer either of milk, or some sort of wine; and every one seemed to take a refusal as if they had solicited, and had not obtained, an act of kindness. If the French are not the most hospitable people in the world, they have at least the art of appearing so. I speak here only of the peasantry, and from first impressions.

The rent of one of these cottages, of two floors and two rooms on each, is thirty-five livres. They have generally a small garden, and about one hundred yards of common land between the road and the house, on which grows the indispensable walnut or chestnut tree. The windows are glazed, but the glass is usually taken out in summer. The walls are generally sea-stone, but are clothed with grape vines, or other shrubs, which, curling around the casements, render them shady and picturesque. The bread is made of wheat meal, but in some cottages consisted of thin cakes without leven, and made of buck-wheat. Their common beverage is a weak wine, sweet and pleasant to the taste. In some houses it very nearly resembled the good metheglin, very common in the northern counties of England. Eggs, bacon, poultry, and vegetables, seemed in great plenty, and, as I understood, composed the dinners of the peasantry twice a week at least. I was surprised at this evident abundance in a class in which I should not have expected it. Something of it, I fear, must be imputed to the extraordinary profits of the smuggling which is carried on along the coast.

I was pleased to see, that even the horrible Revolution had not banished all religion from Calais. I understood that the church was well attended, and that high mass was as much honoured as hitherto. Every one spoke of the Revolution with execration, and of the Emperor with satisfaction. Bonaparte has certainly gained the hearts of the French people by administering to their national vanity.

Returning home from my walk, I was witness to a singular exhibition in the streets. A crowd had collected around a narrow elevated stage, which, at a distant view, led me to expect the appearance, of my friend Punch. I was not altogether deceived: it was a kind of Bartholomew drama, in which the parts were performed by puppets. It differed only from what I had seen in England by the wit of the speakers, and a kind of design, connexion, and uniformity in the fable. The name of it, as announced by the manager, was, The Convention of Kings against France and Bonaparte.

The puppets, who each spoke in their turn, were, the King of England, the King of Naples, the Emperor of Austria, the Pope, and the Grand Signor. The dialogue was indescribably ridiculous. The piece opened with a council, in which the King of England entreated all his brother sovereigns to declare war against France and the French Emperor, and proceeded to assign some ludicrous reasons as applicable to each. "My contribution to the grand alliance," concludes his Majesty, "shall be in money; both because I have more Louis to spare, and because the best advantage of a rich nation is, that it can purchase others to light its battles!" The Grand Signor approves the proposal, and throws down his cimeter. "I will give my cimeter," says he; "but being a prophet as well as a sovereign, and having such a family of wives, I deem it unseemly to use it myself. Let England take it, and give it to any one who will use it manfully." The Pope, in his turn, gives his blessing. "If the war should succeed, you will have to thank my benediction for the victory; if it should fail, it will be from the efficacy of the blessing that a man of you will be saved alive." The Emperor then asks what is the amount of England's contribution; and his British Majesty throws him a purse. His Imperial Majesty, after feeling the weight, takes up the cimeter of the Grand Signor, and retires. The drama then proceeds to the representation of the different battles of Bonaparte, in all of which it gave him the victory, &c.

After a light dinner, in which with some difficulty I procured fish, and with still more had it dressed in the English mode, I mounted my horse, and proceeded on my journey in the road to Boulogne. I had now my first trial of my Norman horse; he fully answered my expectations, and almost my wishes. He had a leisurely lounging walk, which seemed well suited to an observant traveller. It is well known of Erasmus, that he wrote the best of his works, and made a whole course of the Classics, on horseback; and I have no doubt but that I could have both read and written on the back of my Norman. To make up, however, for this tardiness, he was a good-humoured, patient, and sure-footed beast; but would stretch out his neck now and then to get a passing bite of the wheat which grew by the road side. I wished to get on to Boulogne to sleep, and therefore tried all his paces; but found his trotting scarcely tolerable by human feeling.

The road from Calais, for the first twelve miles, is open and hilly. On each side of the main way is a smaller road, which is the summer, as the other is the winter one. The day being very fine, and not too warm, I enjoyed myself much. I passed many fields in which the country people were making hay: they seemed very merry. The fellow who loaded the cart had a cocked hat, and by his erectness I should have thought to have been a soldier, but that every one who passed me had nearly the same air, and the same hat. Some of the hay-makers called to me, but in such barbarous *patois*, that I could make nothing of them. One company of them, saluting me from a distance, deputed a girl to make known their wishes. Seeing her to be young, and expecting her to be handsome, I checked my horse; but a nearer view correcting my error, and exhibiting her only a coarse masculine wench, I pushed forwards, without waiting her embassy. The peasant women of France work so hard, as to lose every appearance of youth in the face, whilst they retain it in the person; and it is therefore no uncommon thing to see the person of a Venus, and the face of an old monkey. I passed by a set of these labourers sitting under a tree, and taking that repast which, in the North of England, is called "fours," from being usually taken by harvest labourers at that time of the day. The party consisted of about a dozen women and girls, and but one man. I was invited to drink some of their wine, and being by the road side, could not refuse. My horse was led under the tree: I was compelled to dismount, and to share their repast, such as it was. Some money which I offered was refused. I made my choice amongst one of my entertainers, and could do no less than salute her. This produced great noise and merriment, and gave free reins to French levity and coquetry; in a word, I was obliged to salute them all. My favourite and first choice gave me her hand on my departure: she might have sat for Prior's Nut-Brown Maid.

The main purpose of my journey being rather to see the manners of the people, than the brick and mortar of the towns, I had formed a resolution to seek the necessary refreshment as seldom as possible at inns, and as often as possible in the houses of the humbler farmers, and the better kind of peasantry. About fifteen miles from Calais my horse and myself were looking out for something of this kind, and one shortly appeared about three hundred yards on the left side of the road. It was a cottage in the midst of a garden, and the whole surrounded by an hedge, which looked delightfully green and refreshing. The garden was all in flower and bloom. The walls of the cottage were robed in the same livery of Nature. I had seen such cottages in Kent and in Devonshire, but in no other part of the world. The inhabitants were simple people, small farmers, having about ten or fifteen acres of land. Some grass was immediately cut for my horse, and the coffee which I produced from my pocket was speedily set before me, with cakes, wine, some meat, and cheese, the French peasantry having no idea of what we call tea. Throwing the windows up, so as to enjoy the scenery and freshness of the garden; sitting upon one chair, and resting a leg upon the other; alternately pouring out my coffee, and reading a pocket-edition of Thomson's Seasons, I enjoyed one of those moments which give a zest to life; I felt happy, and in peace and in love with all around me.

Proceeding upon my journey, two miles on the Calais side of Boulogne I fell in with an overturned chaise, which the postillion was trying to raise. The vehicle was a *chaise de poste*, the ordinary travelling carriage of the country, and a thing in a civilized country wretched beyond conception. It was drawn by three horses, one in the shafts, and one on each side. The postillion had ridden on the one on the driving side; he was a little punch fellow, and in a pair of boots like fire-buckets. The travellers consisted of an old French lady and gentleman; Madame in a high crimped cap, and stiff long whalebone stays. Monsieur informed me very courteously of the cause of the accident, whilst Madame alternately curtsied to me and menaced and scolded the postillion. The French postillions, indeed, are the most intolerable set of beings. They never hesitate to get off their horses, suffer them to go forwards, and follow them very leisurely behind. I saw several instances in which they had suffered the traces to twist round the horses' legs, so that on descending an hill, their escape with life must be a miracle.

I shall briefly observe, now I am upon this subject, that posting is nearly as dear in France as in England. A post in France is six miles, and one shilling and threepence is charged for each horse, and sevenpence for the driver. The price, therefore, for two horses would be three shillings and a penny; but whatever number of persons there may be, a horse is charged for each. The postillions, moreover, expect at least double of what the book of regulations allows them, as matter of right.

I reached Boulogne about sunset, and was much pleased with its vicinity. On each side of the road, and at different distances, from two hundred yards to a mile, were groves of trees, in which were situated some ancient chateaux. Many of them were indeed in ruin from the effects of the Revolution. Upon entering the town, I inquired the way to the Hotel d'Angleterre, which is kept by an Englishman of the name of Parker, Bonaparte having specially exempted him from the edicts respecting aliens. I had a good supper, but an indifferent bed, and the close situation rendered the heat of the night still more oppressive. Mr. Parker himself was absent, and had left the management with a French young woman, who would not suffer me to write uninterrupted, and seemed to take much offence that I did not invite her to take her seat at the supper table. I believe I was the only male traveller in the inn; and flattery, and even substantial gallantry, is so necessary and so natural to French women, that they look to it as their due, and conceive themselves injured when it is withholden.

CHAP. V.

*Boulogne—Dress of the Inhabitants—The Pier—Theatre—Caution in the Exchange of Money—Beautiful Landscape, and Conversation With a French Veteran—Character of Mr. Parker's Hotel—Departure, and romantic Road—Fête Champetre in a Village on a hill at Montreuil—Ruined Church and Convent.*

I had heard so bad a report of Boulogne, as to be agreeably surprised when I found it so little deserving it. I spent the greater part of a day in it with much pleasure, and but that I wished to get to Paris, should have continued longer.

Boulogne is very agreeably situated, and the views from the high grounds on each side are delightful. The landscape from the ramparts is not to be exceeded, but is not seen to advantage except when there is high water in the river. There is an evident mixture of strangers and natives amongst the inhabitants. There are many resident English, who have been nationalized by express edict, or the construction of the law. I heard it casually mentioned, that these were not the most respectable class of inhabitants, though many of them are rich, and all of them are active. The English and French women, whom I met with in the streets, were each dressed in their peculiar fashion; the English women as they dress in the country towns of England; the French without hats, with close caps, and cloaks down to the feet. This fashion I found to be peculiar to Boulogne and its promenade. The town is, upon the whole, clean, lively, brisk, and flourishing; the houses are in good repair, and many others were building.

I walked down to the pier, and my conclusion was, that the English Ministry were mad when they attempted any thing against Boulogne. The harbour appeared to me impregnable. I must confess, however, that the French appeared to me equally mad, in expecting any thing from their flotilla. Three English frigates would sink the whole force at Boulogne in the open sea. The French seem to know this; yet, to amuse the populace, and to play upon the fears of the English Ministry, the farce is kept up, and daily reports are made by the Commandant of the state of the flotilla. There is a delightful walk on the beach, which is a flat strand of firm sand, as far as the tide reaches. In the summer evenings when the tide serves, this is the favourite promenade this is likewise the parade, as the soldiers are occasionally here exercised.

There is a tolerable theatre, but the dramatic corps are not stationary. They were not in the town whilst I was there, so that I can speak of their merits only by report. One of the actresses was highly spoken of, and had indeed reached the reward of her eminence; having been called to the Parisian stage. Bonaparte is notoriously, perhaps politically, attached to the drama, and is no sooner informed of any good performer on a provincial stage, than he issues his command for his appearance and engagement at Paris.

The principal church at Boulogne is a good and respectable structure, and I learned with much satisfaction and some surprise, that on the Sabbath at least it was crowded. The

12

people of Boulogne execrate the Revolution, and avert from all mention and memory of it, and not without reason, as their environs have been in some degree spoiled by its excesses. Several miles on the road from Boulogne, those sad monuments of the popular phrensy, ruined chateaux, and churches converted into stables or granaries, force the memory back upon those melancholy times, when the property and religion of a nation became the but of bandits and atheists. May the world itself perish, before such an era shall return or become general!

I had received from an American house in London some bills on a mercantile house at Boulogne; a very convenient method, and which I would therefore recommend to other travellers, as they hereby save very considerably, such bills being usually given at some advantage in favour of those who purchase them by coin. Bills on Boulogne, Bourdeaux, and Havre, are always to be had of the American brokers, either in London or in New York. One advantage in this exchange is, that bills may be had of any date, in which case you may suit the occasions, and put the discount into your own pocket. My bill on Boulogne was for 3000 francs, about 130*l.* English. I received it in Louis d'ors and écus. In the progress of my journey, several of the Louis were refused, as deficient in weight, and I was advised in future never to take a Louis without seeing that it was weight. The French coin is indeed in a very bad state, which here, as elsewhere, is attributed to the Jews.

On the Paris side of Boulogne is a landscape and walk of most exquisite beauty. The river, after some smaller meanders, takes a wide reach through a beautiful vale, and shortly after flows into the sea through two hills, which open as it were to receive it. I walked along the banks to have a better view, and got into converse with a soldier, who had been in the battle of Marengo. He gave me a very lively account of the conduct of that extraordinary man, the French Emperor, in this grand event of his life. His expression was, that he looked over the battle as if looking upon a chess-board: that he made it a rule never to engage personally, till he saw the whole plan of the battle in execution; that he would then ride alternately to each division, and encourage them by fighting awhile with them: that he visited all the sick and wounded soldiers the day after the battle, inquired into the nature of their wound, where and how it was received; and if there were any circumstances of peculiar merit or peculiar distress, noted it down, and invariably acted upon this memorandum: that he punished adultery in a soldier's wife, if they were both in the camp, by the death of the woman; if the offending was not in the field, and therefore not within the reach of a court-martial, the soldier had a divorce on simple proof of the offence before any mayor or magistrate. I demanded of this veteran, pointing to the flotilla, when the Emperor intended to invade England? He perceived the smile which accompanied this question, and instantaneously, with a fierce look of suspicion and resolution, demanded of me my passport. Though the abruptness of his conduct startled me, I could not but regard him with some admiration. A long, thin, spare figure of 55, was so sensible of the honour of his country, as to take fire even at a jest at it as at a personal insult. It is to this spirit that France owes half her victories.

As soon as the heat of the day had declined, having satisfied my curiosity as to Boulogne, I called for my bill and my horse, intending to get on to Montreuil, where I had fixed upon sleeping. My bill was extravagant to a degree; a circumstance I imputed to the want of some due attentions to Madame. These kind of people have always the revenge in their own hands. As I did not see Mr. Parker, I know not whether to recommend his inn or not. He has some excellent Burgundy, but the charges are high, the attendance not good, and the situation in summer close and stifling. Madame, however, is a very pretty woman, and seems a very good-humoured one, if her expectations are answered. She is a true French woman, however, and expects gallantry even from a weary traveller.

I found the road improve much as I advanced; the country became more enclosed, and bore a strong resemblance to the most cultivated parts of England. The cherry trees standing in the midst of the corn had a very pretty effect; the fields had the appearance of gardens, and some of the gardens had the wildness of the field. The season was evidently more advanced than in England; there were more fruits and flowers, and the bloom was more bossy and luxuriant. Several smaller roads led from the main road, and the spires of the village churches, as seen in the side landscape, rising above the tops of the trees, invited the fancy to combine some rural images, and weave itself at least an imaginary Arcadia. The persons I met or overtook upon the road were not altogether in unison with what I must call the romance of the scene. Every carter drove his vehicle in a cocked-hat, and the women had all wooden shoes. Boys and girls of twelve years old were in rags, which very ill covered them. Nor was there any of the briskness visible on a high road in England. A single cart, and a waggon, were all the vehicles that I saw between Boulogne and Abbeville. In England, in the same space, I should have seen a dozen, or score.

Not being pressed for time, the beauty of a scene at some little distance from the road-side tempted me to enter into a bye-lane, and take a nearer view of it. A village church, embosomed in a chesnut wood, just rose above the trees on the top of a hill; the setting sun was on its casements, and the foliage of the wood was burnished by the golden reflection. The distant hum of the village green was just audible; but not so the French horn, which echoed in full melody through the groves. Having rode about half a mile through a narrow sequestered lane, which strongly reminded me of the half-green and half-trodden bye-roads in Warwickshire, I came to the bottom of the hill, on the brow and summit of which the village and church were situated. I now saw whence the sound of the horn proceeded. On the left of the road was an ancient chateau situated in a park, or very extensive meadow, and ornamented as well by some venerable trees, as by a circular fence of flowering shrubs, guarded on the outside by a paling on a raised mound. The park or meadow having been newly mown, had an air at once ornamented and natural. A party of ladies were collected under a patch of trees situated in the middle of the lawn. I stopt at the gate to look at them, thinking myself unperceived: but in the same moment the gate was opened to me by a gentleman and two ladies, who were walking the round. An explanation was now necessary, and was accordingly given. The gentleman informed me upon his part, that the chateau belonged to Mons. St. Quentin, a Member of the French Senate, and a Judge of the District; that he had a party of friends with him upon the occasion of his lady's birth-day, and that they were about to begin dancing; that Mons. St. Quentin would highly congratulate himself on my accidental arrival. One of the ladies, having previously apologized and left us, had seemingly explained to Mons. St. Quentin the main circumstance belonging to me, for he now appeared, and repeated the invitation in his own person. The ladies added their kind importunities. I dismounted, gave my horse to a servant in waiting, and joined this happy and elegant party, for such it really was.

I had now, for the first time, an opportunity of forming an opinion of French beauty, the assemblage of ladies being very numerous, and all of them most elegantly dressed. Travelling, and the imitative arts, have given a most surprising uniformity to all the fashions of dress and ornament; and, whatever may be said to the contrary, there is a very slight difference between the scenes of a French and English polite assembly. If any thing, however, be distinguishable, it is more in degree than in substance. The French fashions, as I saw them here, differed in no other point from what I had seen in London, but in degree. The ladies were certainly more exposed about the necks, and their hair was dressed with more fancy; but the form was in almost every thing the same. The most elegant novelty was a hat, which doubled up like a fan, so that the ladies carried it in their hands. There were more coloured than white muslins; a variety which had a pretty effect amongst the trees and flowers. The same observation applies to the gentlemen. Their dresses were made as in England; but the pattern of the cloth, or some appendage to it, was different. One gentleman, habited in a grass-coloured silk coat, had very much the appearance of Beau Mordecai in the farce: the ladies, however, seemed to admire him, and in some conversation with him I found him, in despite of his coat, a very well-informed man. There were likewise three or four fancy dresses; a Dian, a wood-nymph, and a sweet girl playing upon a lute, habited according to a picture of Calypso by David. On the whole, there was certainly more fancy, more taste, and more elegance, than in an English party of the same description; though there were not so many handsome women as would have been the proportion of such an assembly in England.

A table was spread handsomely and substantially under a very large and lofty marquee. The outside was very prettily painted for the occasion—Venus commemorating her birth from the ocean. The French manage these things infinitely better than any other nation in the world. It was necessary, however, for the justice of the compliment, that the Venus should be a likeness of Madame St. Quentin, who was neither very young nor very handsome. The painter, however, got out of the scrape very well.

A small party accompanied me into the village, which was lively, and had some very neat houses. The peasantry, both men and women, had hats of straw; a manufactory which Mons. St. Quentin had introduced. A boy was reading at a cottage-door. I had the curiosity to see the book. It was a volume of Marmontel. His mother came out, invited us into the house, and in the course of some conversation, produced some drawings by this youth; they were very simple, and very masterly. The ladies purchased them at a good price. He had attained this excellence without a master, and Mons. St. Quentin, as we were informed, had been so pleased with him, as to take him into his house. His temper and manners, however, were not in unison with his taste, and his benefactor had been compelled to restore him to his mother, but still intended to send him to study at Paris. The boy's countenance was a direct lie to Lavater; his air was heavy, and absolutely without intelligence. Mons. St. Quentin had dismissed him his house on account of a very malignant sally of passion: a horse having thrown him by accident, the young demon took a knife from his pocket, and deliberately stabbed him three several times. Such was a peasant boy, now seemingly enveloped in the interesting simplicity of Marmontel. How inconsistent is what is called character!

I had a sweet ride for the remaining way to Montreuil by moon-light, accompanied by two gentlemen on horseback, who lived in that town. They related to me many melancholy incidents during the revolutionary period. Montreuil was formerly distributed into five parishes, and had five churches; but the people doubtless thinking that five was too many for the religion of the town, destroyed the other four, and sold the best part of the materials. Accordingly, when I entered the town, my eye was caught by a noble ruin, which upon inquiry I found to be the church of Notre Dame. This ruin is beautiful beyond description. The pillars which remain are noble, and the capitals and carving rich to a degree. It is astonishing to me that any reasonable beings, the inhabitants of a town, could thus destroy its chief ornament; but in the madness of the revolutionary fanatics, the sun itself would have been plucked from Heaven, if they could have reached it. I was sincerely happy to learn that religion had returned, and that there was a general inclination to subscribe for the repair, or rather rebuilding, of Notre Dame.

My friends took leave of me after recommending to me an inn kept by two sisters, the name of which I have forgotten. They were so handsome as to resemble English women, and what is very uncommon in this class of people in France, were totally without rouge. Whilst my supper was preparing, I had a moon-light walk round the town. The situation of it is at once commanding and beautiful. The ruins of a chateau, seen under the light of the moon, improved the scenery, and was another memento of the execrable Revolution. There are a number of pretty houses, and some of them substantial. One of them belonged to one of the gentlemen who accompanied me from Mons. St. Quentin's, and was his present residence, being all that remained to him of a noble property in the vicinity. This property had been sold by the nation, and the recovery of it had become impossible, though the gentleman was in tolerable favour with the government. Bonaparte had answered one of this gentleman's memorials by subscribing it with a sentence in his own writing: "We cannot re-purchase the nation." This gentleman spoke highly, but perhaps unjustly, of the vigour of Bonaparte's government, of his inflexible love of justice, and his personal attention to the administration. I compelled him, however, to acknowledge, that in his own immediate concerns, the justice of the French Chief was not proof against his passions. I mentioned the Duke of Enghien; the gentleman pushed on his horse, and begged me to say no more of the matter.

Upon my return I had an excellent supper, and what was still more welcome, a bed which reminded me of those at an English coffee-house.

### CHAP. VI.

*Departure from Montreuil—French Conscripts—Extreme Youth—Excellent*
*Roads—Country Labourers—Court for the Claims*
*of Emigrants—Abbeville—Companion on the Road—Amiens.*

As I wished to reach Paris as soon as possible, I had ordered the chambermaid to call me at an early hour in the morning; but was awakened previous to the appointed time by some still earlier travellers—a very numerous detachment of conscripts, who were on their march for the central *depôt* of the department. The greater part of them were boys, and were merry and noisy in a manner characteristic of the French youth. Seeing me at the window, one of them struck up a very lively *reveillée*, and was immediately joined by others who composed their marching band. They were attended, and their baggage carried, by a peculiar kind of cart—a platform erected on wheels, and on which they ascended when fatigued. The vehicles were prepared, the horses harnessed, and the young conscripts impatiently waiting for the word to march.

When I came down into the inn-yard, no one was stirring in the house except the ostler, who, upon my mentioning the component items of my entertainment, very fairly, as I thought, reckoned them up, and received the amount, taking care to remind me of the chambermaid. Having with some difficulty likewise procured from him a glass of milk, I mounted my horse, and followed the conscripts, who, with drum and fife, were merrily but regularly marching before me. The regularity of the march continued only till they got beyond the town, and down the hill, when the music ceased, the ranks broke, and every one walked or ran as he pleased. As they were somewhat too noisy for a meditating traveller, I put my horse to his mettle, and soon left them at a convenient distance.

I must cursorily observe, that the main circumstance which struck me in this detachment, was the extreme youth of the major part. I saw not a man amongst them, and some of them had an air the most perfectly childish. Bonaparte is said to prefer these young recruits. No army in Europe would have admitted them, with the exception of the French.

The road was truly excellent, though hilly, and indeed so continued till within a few miles of Abbeville. The present Emperor acts so far upon the system of the ancient monarchy, and considers the goodness of the highways as the most important and most immediate object of the administration; accordingly, the roads in France are still better than under the Bourbons, as Bonaparte sees every thing with his own eyes. Nothing, indeed, is wanting to quick travelling in France, but English drivers and English carriages. How would a mail-coach roll upon such a road! The French postillions, and even the French horses, such as I met on the road, have a kind of activity without progress—the postillions are very active in cracking their whips over their heads, and the horses shuffle about without mending their pace.

I passed several country labourers, men and women, going to their daily toil. I was informed by one of them, that he worked in the hay-field, and earned six-and-thirty sous (1*s.* 6*d.*) a day; that the wages for mowers were fifty sous (2*s.* 1*d.*), and two bottles of wine or cyder; that his wife had fourteen sous and her food; and boys and children old enough to rake, from six to twelve sous. He paid 25 livres annually for the rent of his cottage. When he had to support himself, he breakfasted on bread, and a glass or more of strong wine or brandy; dined on bread and cheese, and supped on bread and an apple. He wore leather shoes, except in wet weather, when he wore *sabots*, which cost about twelve sous per pair.

I passed more *chateaux* in ruins, and others shut up and forsaken. Some of them were very prettily situated, in patches of trees and amidst corn-fields. Several, as I understood, belonged to emigrants, whom Bonaparte had recalled by name, but who had not as yet returned. I learned with some satisfaction, that some shew of justice was still necessary. Where the property of the emigrants is unsold, and still in the hands of the nation, the emigrated proprietor is not totally without a chance of restitution. If he can come forwards, and prove, in a court established for the purpose, that he has merely been absent; that his absence was not without sufficient reasons; that he has not taken up arms against France; and finally, had returned as soon as he possessed the means—under these circumstances, the lands are restored. Even his children may succeed where himself shall fail. Upon proof of infancy at the time of emigration, and that they have at no time borne arms against the empire, the lands are not unfrequently decreed to them, even when the father's claim has been rejected.

I reached Bernay to breakfast, and, for the first time in France, met with a surly host and a sour hostess. The bread being stale, salt, and bitter, I desired it to be changed. The host obeyed, so far as to carry it out of the room and bring it in again. It was in vain, however, that I insisted upon the identity, till I desired him to bring what he had removed, and to compare it with what he had brought. He then flatly told me, that I must either have that or none; that it was as good bread as any in France, and that he intended to eat it for his own breakfast. His wife came in, hearing my raised voice, and maintained her husband's assertions very stoutly. For the sake of peace, I found it necessary to submit. He is a true hero who can support a contest with a man and his wife. The girl who waited on me seemed made of kinder materials. She laughed with much archness when I shewed her the bread, and its vigorous resistance to the edge of my knife. She was born in Musilius, and told me, with true French coquetry, that her sisters were as handsome as herself. She mentioned some English name (that of a valet, I suppose), and asked me if I knew him in London. If I should hereafter meet him, I was to remind him of Bernay. The charges, contrary to my expectations, were as moderate as the breakfast was indifferent; and the host did me the honour to wish me good morning. The hostess, however, was inflexibly sour, and saw me depart without a word, or even a salutation.

I had a most unpleasant ride to Abbeville, the heat of the day being extreme, and the road totally without any shelter. I imagined, however, that the heat was less oppressive than heat of the same intensity in England; but I know not whether this difference was any thing but imaginary. In foreign countries, we are so much upon the hunt for novelty, and so well predisposed to find it, that in things not strongly nor immediately the objects of sense, our impressions are not altogether to be trusted.

Abbeville, which I reached in good time for the *table d'hôte*, which is held on every market-day, is a populous but a most unpleasant town. The inhabitants are stated to exceed 22,000; but I do not conceive that they can amount to one half of that number. The town has a most ruinous appearance, from the circumstance of many of the houses being built with wood; and by the forms of the windows and the doors, some of them must be very ancient. There are two or three manufactories of cloth, but none of them were in a flourishing condition. I went to visit that of Vanrobais, established by Louis XIV. and which still continues, though in ruins. The buildings are upon a very large scale; but too much was attempted for them to execute any thing in a workmanlike manner. There are different buildings for every different branch of the manufacture. I cannot but think, however, that they would have succeeded better if they had consulted the principle of the sub-division of labour. A man who is both a weaver and a spinner, will certainly not be both as good a weaver and as good a spinner, as another who is only a spinner or only a weaver: he will not have the same dexterity, and therefore will not do the same work. No business is done so well as that which is the sole object of attention. I saw likewise a manufactory of carpets, which seemed more flourishing. In the cloth manufactory, the earnings of the working manufacturers are about 36 sous per diem (1s.6d.): in the carpet manufactories, somewhat more. The cloths, as far as I am a judge, seemed to me even to exceed those of England; but the carpets are much inferior. From some unaccountable reason, however, the cloths were much dearer than English broad cloth of the same quality. Whence does this happen, in a country where provisions are so much cheaper? Perhaps from that neglect of the sub-division of labour which I have above noticed.

Abbeville, like all the other principal towns through which I passed, bore melancholy marks of the Revolution. The handsome church which stood in the market-place is in ruins—scarcely a stone remains on the top of another. Many of the best houses were shut up, and others of the same description, evidently inhabited by people for whom they were not built. In many of them, one room only was inhabited; and in others, the second and third floors turned into granaries. Indeed, along the whole road from Abbeville to Paris, are innumerable *chateaux*, which are now only the cells of beggars, or of the lowest kind of peasantry.

An officer who was going to Amiens, joined company with me on the road to Pequigny, and, like every Frenchman of this class, became communicative almost in the same instant in which we had exchanged salutes. I found, however, that he knew nothing, except in his own profession; and I very strongly suspect, that he even here gave me some details of battles in which he had never been, or at least he made two or three geographical mistakes, for which I cannot otherwise account. He made no scruple of moving the Rhine a few degrees easterly; and constructed a bridge over the Adige without the help of the mason. I have not unfrequently, indeed, been surprized at the unaccountable ignorance betrayed by this class of men. It is to be hoped, that in another age this will pass away. My companion, however, had a good-humour which compensated for his ignorance; he alternately talked, sung, and dismounted from his horse to speak to every peasant girl who met us on the road; he seemed at home with every one, and made the time pass agreeably enough. He sung, at my request, the Marseillois, and sung it with such emphasis, energy, and attitude, as to make me sincerely repent the having called forth such a deafening exhibition of his powers. Though one or two travellers passed us whilst he was thus exhibiting, my gentleman was not in the slightest degree discomposed, but continued his song, his attitudes, and his grimaces, as if he were in the midst of a wood.

After a very long journey, in which my little Norman had performed to admiration, I reached Amiens about eight o'clock, on the sweetest summer evening imaginable. The aspect of Amiens, as it is approached by the road, resembles Canterbury—the cathedral rising above the town—the town, as it were, gathering around it as its parent and protector. My companion would not leave me till he had seen me to the inn, the *Iotel d'Angleterre*, when he took a farewell of me as if we had been intimate for years, and I have no doubt, thought no more of me after he had turned the corner of the street. These attentions, however, are not the less pleasing, and answer their purpose as well as if they were more permanent. Having ordered my supper, and seen my horse duly provided for, I walked through the town, which is clean, lively, and in many respects resembling towns of the third rate in England. I visited the cathedral, which pleased me much; but has been so often described, that I deem it unnecessary to say more of it. It was built by the English in the time of Henry VI. and the regency of the Duke of Bedford, and has much of the national taste of that people, and those times. Though strictly Gothic, it is light, and very tastefully ornamented: it infinitely exceeds any cathedral in England, with the exception of Westminster Abbey. I went to see likewise the *Chateau d'Eau*, the machine for supplying Amiens with water. There is nothing more than common in it, and the purpose would be answered better by pipes and a steam-engine. It excited one observation which I have since frequently made—that the French, with all their parade of science and ostentation of institutions, are still a century behind England in real practical knowledge. My Tour in France has at least taught me one lesson—never to be deceived by high-sounding names and pompous designations. I have not visited their schools for nothing. The French talk; the English act. A steady plodding Englishman will build an house, while a Frenchman is laying down rules for it. There is more of this idle pedantry in France than in any country on the face of the globe: every thing is done with science, and nothing with knowledge.

Walking through the market-place, my attention was taken by an unusual bustle—the erecting of scaffolds, booths, and other similar preparations. I learned, upon inquiry, that the half-yearly fair was to be held on the following day; a piece of information which confirmed my previous intention of passing that day at Amiens.

Upon returning to the inn, I had a supper as comfortable as any I had ever sat down to, even in England. The landlord, at my particular request, took his seat with me at table. He complained bitterly of the oppression of the taxes, and more particularly of their uncertainty, which was so indeterminate, according to his assertions, that the collectors took what they pleased, and employed their offices as means of favour, or to gratify their personal piques. One of the collectors of Amiens, it seems, was likewise an inn-keeper, who availed himself of the power of his office to harass his rival. There is no appeal, as long as the collector is faithful to the government, and pays in what he receives. The manner in which defaulters are treated, is peculiar to the French government. If the sum assessed be not paid within the appointed time, a soldier is billeted at the house of the defaulter, and another is daily added till the arrear be cleared. The greater part of the taxes have been imposed during the strong days of the Revolution; and as they are sufficiently productive, and the present government have not the odium of their first institution, they are suffered to continue upon their old foundation—that is to say, upon an infinite number of successive decrees, many of which contradict each other. No one, therefore, knows exactly what he has to pay, and any one may be made to pay according to the caprice of the collector.

## CHAP. VII.

*General Character of the Town—Public Walk—Gardens—Half-yearly Fair—Gaming Houses—Table d'Hôtes—English at Amiens—Expence of Living.*

THE noise of the people collecting for the fair, and the consequent bustle of the inn, awoke me at an early hour in the morning; and after a breakfast which reminded me of England, I sallied forth to see the town and the lions. A vast multitude of people had assembled from the surrounding country, and were collected around the several booths. The day was fine, the bells were ringing, and the music playing; every one was dressed in their holiday clothes, and every one seemed to have a happy and careless face, suitable to the festivity of the occasion.

Amiens is most delightfully situated, the country around being highly cultivated. It is, in every respect, one of the cleanest towns in France; and the frequent visits and long residence of Englishmen, have produced a very sensible alteration in the manner of living amongst the inhabitants. Though some of the houses are very ancient, and the streets are narrow, it has not the ruinous nor close appearance of the other towns on the Paris road. It has been lately newly paved; and there is something, of the nature of a parish-rate for keeping it clean, and in summer for watering the streets.

Though Amiens has suffered very considerably by the war, it has still, in appearance at least, an extensive trade. The manufactures are of the same kind as those at Abbeville. Besides their cloths, however, they work up a considerable quantity of camblets, callimancoes, and baizes, chiefly red and spotted, for domestic consumption. They were in great distress for wool, and could procure none but by land-carriage from Spain, Portugal, and Flanders. Upon examining two or three of their articles, I thought them very dear, but very good. I visited two or three of their manufactories, and upon inquiring for others, was informed that they had been shut up. The effect of the war had been, to raise prices to double their former rate: every one expressed an anxious wish for peace, and imputed the continuance of the war to the English Ministry.

The general character of the people of Amiens is, that they are lively, good-humoured, and less infected by the revolutionary contagion than any town in France: as many of them as I had an opportunity of conversing with, spoke with due detestation of jacobinism, and with an equal wise submission to the present order of things. Besides the native inhabitants, there are many foreign residents, and some English. As these are in general in good circumstances, they have usually the best houses in the town, and live in the substantial style of their respective countries. The English denizens very well understand that they are constantly under the eye of the French government, and its spies: they live, therefore, as much as possible in public; and in their balls, and dinners, and entertainments, have a due mixture of French visitants. Several of them avoid this restraint by passing for Americans; but the detection of this deception is most severely punished. The English have contrived, however, to procure both the good will and the good word of the people of Amiens, and even the French government seems to regard them with peculiar favour.

Every considerable town in France has its public walk, and Amiens has one or more of singular beauty; but being situated in an unenclosed country, and amongst corn-fields, its private walks are still more frequented than its ancient promenade. I was informed that the English had brought these private walks into general fashion, and I considered it as an additional proof of their good sense and natural taste.

The multitude of people assembled from every part of the province, gave me an opportunity of seeing the national costume of the peasantry. The habits of the men did not appear to me so various, and so novel, as those of the women. The greater part of the former had three-cocked hats, some of straw, some of pasteboard, and some of beaver; jackets, red, yellow, and blue; and breeches of the same fancy colours. The women were dressed in a variety both of shape and colour, which defies all description. When seen from a distance, the assembly had a very picturesque appearance: the sun shining on the various

19

colours, gave them the appearance of so many flowers. The general features of the fair did not differ much from the fairs in England and America. There were two streets completely filled with booths: the market-place was occupied with shows, and temporary theatres. I observed, however, two or three peculiar national amusements; one of them called the *Mats de Cocagne*, the other the *Mats de Beaupré*. The *Mats de Cocagne* are long poles, some of them thirty feet in height, well greased, and erected perpendicularly. At the top of them is suspended by a string, a watch, a shirt, or other similar articles, which become the prize of the fortunate adventurer who can ascend and reach them. A few sous are paid to the proprietor of the *mat*, for the chance of gaining the prize; it is the fault, therefore, of the proprietor, if the *mat* be not so well greased as to render the ascent almost impossible. I saw many fruitless attempts made: one fellow had nearly gained the top, and was within reach of the prize; he stretched his hand out to take it, and having by this act diminished his hold, came down with the most frightful rapidity. The crowd laughed; and another adventurer, nothing dismayed, succeeded him in the attempt, and in the failure. The prize, however, was at length obtained; but the adventurer, I should think, had not much cause to congratulate himself on his good luck. His descent was of a rapidity which caused the blood to gush out of his mouth and his nose, and for some time, at least, frightened the multitude from repeating the same sport.

The *Mats de Beaupré* are upon the same principle; they are soaped poles, laid horizontally, but very high from the ground. At the further extremity of them are the same prizes, and which are gained upon the same condition—the men to walk over, the women to scramble over them in any manner which they might deem best. To break the violence of the fall, the ground immediately under the poles was thickly laid with straw. Several women, and innumerable girls, made an attempt to gain the prize at these *Mats de Beaupré*, and in the course of their efforts had some tumbles, which much delighted the mob. Indeed, this kind of sport seemed peculiarly intended for the females: the men seemed to prefer the *Cocagnes*.

The chief enjoyment of the multitude, however, seemed to be dancing. Several scaffolds, with benches rising one above another, were erected in every part of the town: these were the orchestras, which, as far as I saw, were supported by the voluntary contributions of the companies which danced to their music. A subscription was always made after every dance, and each dancer subscribed a sous. The ladies, I believe, were excused by the payment of their partners. The dancing was excellent, and the music by no means contemptible.

The shows were much of the same kind as those in Bartholomew fair, in London, and which travel from town to town during the summer in America. The mountebanks and merry-andrews appeared more dexterous and more humorous. One of the former seeing me, entreated the crowd to make way for me; and when I turned my back, "Nay, my good friend," said he, "do not mistake me. I have no intention of asking you for the money which you owe to me for your last cure; you are very welcome to it. I delight in doing good. I am paid sufficiently by your recovery. If you choose, however, to remember, my young man"— The merry-andrew was here at my side, and I deemed it most prudent to drop a few sous into his cap, and effect my escape. The crowd understood the jest, and laughed heartily. One of them, however, of more decent appearance, made me a very pleasing apology, repeating at the same time a French proverb—that a pope and a mountebank were above all law.

Amongst the commodities exhibited for sale, I was agreeably surprised to find two or more booths well supplied with English and French books; and my surprise was still greater, to find that the former had many purchasers. I took up several of them, and found them to be English Gazetteers, Tours in England, Wales, Scotland; Travels in America, Dictionaries, and Grammars. From some cause or other, the English seem in particular favour in and about Amiens, and Lord Cornwallis is still remembered with respect and affection.

There, were other booths which excited less pleasing reflections; these were the temporary gaming tables, the admission to which was from six to twelve sous. I had the curiosity to enter one of them: it was already full. One party was at eager play, and others were waiting to succeed them. I could make nothing of the game, only that it was one of chance, and that the winnings and losings were determined in every three casts. I saw a decent young man take off and stake his neckcloth: fortune favoured him, and he had the uncommon fortitude to retire, and play no more. There was another booth of rather a singular kind—a temporary pawnbroker's, and who appeared to have a good brisk trade.

My attention, however, was more peculiarly attracted by a marquee, open on all sides, and with an elevated floor: a chair, covered with green velvet, was here placed, and occupied by a man of much apparent gravity. I found, upon inquiry, that this was the president, judge, or magistrate of the fair; that he was elected by votes of the booth-holders, and determined all disputes on the spot; that his authority was supported by the police, and his sentence enforced by the municipality. He was a portly man, wore a three-cocked hat, and an old scarlet cloak, which had served the same purpose time out of mind.

I returned to my hotel to dinner; and being informed that there was a *table d'hôte*, and that it would be very numerously attended, I preferred it to dining in my own apartment, and at the appointed hour took my seat. The company was indeed numerous—men, women, girls, and children; officers of the army, exhibitors of wild beasts, actors and actresses of the booth-theatres. A separate table was set for the officers of the army. I had here a specimen of the manners of the French revolutionary officers. A party of them, to the number of fifteen or twenty, had already placed themselves at table, when the commandant, or at least a superior officer, entered the room. They all immediately got up to make room for him, and handed him a chair in a manner the most servile and fawning. "I hope I disturb no one," said he, at the same time throwing himself into the chair, but not offering to move his hat. He continued during the whole of the dinner the same disgusting superiority, and the subordinate officers several times called out silence to the adjoining table, that they might better hear the vapid remarks of their commander. The waiters, and even the whole *table d'hôte* seemed in great awe of these military gentlemen; and one fellow excused himself for leaving a plate before me by hastily alleging that the commander was looking around him for something. I was still more disgusted by one of the officers rising, and proposing this important gentleman's health to both tables; and my surprise was greater by recognizing, in the tone of this proposal, the barbarous twang of an Irishman. Some of the French regiments are half filled with these Irish renegades. I cannot speak of them with any patience, as I cannot conceive any voluntary degradation more contemptible, than that of passing from any thing British or American into any thing French or Italian. I have a respect for the Irish in the German service; they are still members of a people like themselves. I say not this in contempt of the French themselves, but of the English or Irish become French.

In the evening I went to one of the theatres, accompanied by an English physician, with whom I dined at the *table d'hôte*. This gentleman came into France after the peace of Amiens, and was of course included in the number detained by the French Emperor. Having some friends in the Institute, they had drawn up a memorial in his favour, in which they represented him, and very justly, as a man of science, who had come into France to compare the English and French system of medicine, and whose researches had already excited much interest and inquiry amongst the French physicians. This memorial being delivered into the hands of the Emperor himself, was subscribed by him in the following words: "Let him remain in France during the war, on his parole that he will not leave the French territories, and will have no correspondence with England."

The performance at the theatre was too contemptible for mention, and in the pantomime, or rather spectacle, became latterly so indelicate, that I found it necessary to withdraw. I should hope that the performances are not always of the same character: perhaps something must be allowed for the occasion. The French, however, have no idea of humour as separated from indecencies. In this respect they might take a very useful lesson from the English. The English excel in pantomime as much as the French in comedy.

Dr. M—— returned to supper with me, and gave me some useful information. Every trace of the Revolution is rapidly vanishing at Amiens. Religion has resumed her influence: the cathedral is very well attended, but auricular confession is not usual. The clergy of Amiens, however, are very poor, having lost all their immense possessions, and having nothing but the national stipend. The cathedral had been repaired by public subscription. The poor are sent to the armies. There were no imposts but those paid to the government.

Amiens is still a very cheap town for permanent residence, though the war has very seriously affected it. A good house may be rented for thirty pounds per annum, the taxes upon the mere house being about a Louis. Mutton seldom exceeds threepence English money per pound, and beef is usually somewhat cheaper. Poultry of all kinds is in great plenty, and cheap: fowls, ducks, &c. about two shillings per couple. A horse at livery, half a Louis per week; two horses, all expences included, a Louis and two livres. Board and lodging in a genteel house, five-and-twenty Louis annually. Dr. M—— agreed with me, that for three hundred a year, a family might keep their carriage and live in comfort, in Amiens and its neighbourhood. I must not forget another observation; the towns in France are cheaper than the villages. The consumption of meat in the latter is not sufficient to induce the butchers to kill often; the market, therefore, is very ill supplied, and consequently the prices are dear. A few miles from a principal town, you cannot have a leg of mutton without paying for the whole sheep.

A stranger may live at an inn at Amiens for about five shillings, English money, a day. The wine is good, and very cheap; and a daily ordinary, or *table d'hôte*, is kept at the *Hotel d'Angleterre*. Breakfast is charged one livre, dinner three, and supper one: half a livre for coffee, and two livres for lodging; but if you remain a week, ten livres for the whole time. The hotels, of which there are two, are as good as those of Paris, and lodgings are far more reasonable. A *restaurateur* has very lately set up in a very grand style, but the population of the town will scarcely support him. The company at the *table d'hôte* usually consists of officers, of whom there is always a multitude in the neighbourhood of Amiens. Some of them, as I was informed, are very pleasant agreeable men; whilst others are ruffians, and have the manners of jacobins.

## CHAP. VIII.
*French and English Roads compared—Gaiety of French*
*Labourers—Breteuil—Apple-trees in the midst of Corn-fields—Beautiful*
*Scenery—Cheap Price of Land in France—Clermont—Bad Management*
*of the French Farmers—Chantilly—Arrival at Paris.*

I left Amiens early on the following morning, intending to reach Clermont in good time.

The roads now became very indifferent, but the scenery was much improved. I could not but compare the prospect of a French road with one of the great roads of England. It is impossible to travel a mile on an English road without meeting or overtaking every species of vehicle. The imagination of a traveller, if as susceptible as a traveller's imagination should be, has thus a constant food for its exercise; it accompanies these several groups to their home or destination, and calls before its view the busy market, the quiet village, the blazing hearth, the returning husband, and the welcoming wife. No man is fit for a traveller who cannot while away his time in such creations of his fancy. I pity the traveller from my heart, who in a barren or uniform road, has no other occupation but to count the mile-stones, and find every mile as long as the three preceding. Let such men become drivers to stage-coaches, but let them not degrade the name of travellers by assuming it to themselves.

On a French road, there is more necessity than objects for this exercise of the imagination. A French road is like a garden in the old French style. It is seldom either more or less than a straight line ruled from one end of the kingdom to the other. There are no angles, no curvatures, no hedges; one league is the exact counterpart of another; instead of hedges, are railings, and which are generally in a condition to give the country not only a naked, but even a slovenly, ruinous appearance. Imagine a road made over an heath, and each side of it fenced off by a railing of old hurdles, and you will have no imperfect idea of a French great road. Within a mile, indeed, of the neighbourhood of a principal town, the prospect usually varies and improves. The road is then planted on each side, and becomes a beautiful avenue through lofty and shady trees. This description, however, will only apply to the great roads. Some of the cross and country roads, as I shall hereafter have occasion to mention, not only equal, but greatly exceed, even the English roads, in natural beauty and scenery.

In the course of the road between Amiens and Clermont, I had again too frequent opportunity to remark the slovenly management of the French farmers, as compared with those of England, and even with those of America. In America, the farmers are not without a very sufficient excuse. The scarcity of hands, the impossibility of procuring labourers at any price, compel an American farmer to get in his harvest as he can, to collect the crop of one field hastily, and then fly to another. In France there is no such excuse, and therefore there should be no such slovenly waste. Yet in some of the hay-fields which I passed, at least one-fifth *of* the crop was lying scattered on the roads and in the fields. The excuse was, that the cattle would eat it, and that they might as well have it one way as another. It would be folly to say any thing as to such an argument; yet in these very fields the labour was so plentiful and minute, that the greater part of the crop was carried from the fields on the shoulders of the labourers, men, women, and boys. It is difficult to reconcile such inconsistencies.

In such of the fields as I saw carts, the most severe labour seemed to be allotted to the share of the women. They were the pitchers, and performed this labour with a very heavy, and as it appeared to me, a very awkward fork. Whilst the women were performing this task, two or three fellows, raw-boned, and nearly six feet high, were either very leisurely raking, or perhaps laying at their full length under the new-made stacks. In other fields I saw more pleasing groups. At the sound of a horn like the English harvest horn, the pitchers, the loaders, and every labourer on the spot, left their work, and collected around some tree or hay-cock, to receive their noon refreshment. The indispensable fiddle was never wanting. Even the horses, loosened from the carts, and suffered to feed at liberty, seemed to partake in the general merriment, and looked with erect ears at the fiddler and his dancing group. When, the hour allotted to this relaxation expired, the labourers were again called to the several duties by the summons of the same horn, which was now sounded from the top of the loaded cart, as it had before been sounded under the tree or hay-cock. I had forgotten to mention, that the tree or hay-cock, the appointed place of refreshment, was distinguished by pennants of different coloured ribbons attached to a stick as a flag-staff, and which waving in the wind, under a beautiful midsummer sky, had an effect peculiarly pleasing. As I saw the same spectacle in several fields, I believe it to be national.

Breteuil, which I reached in time for a late breakfast, is a very paltry town; the houses are all built in the ancient style, and bear an unfavourable resemblance to English farm-houses; their gable-ends are turned to the streets, and the chimneys are nearly as large as the roofs. There was no appearance of business, not even of a brisk retail, or of a lively thoroughfare. A crowd collected around us as I entered the inn, as if a decent stranger, travelling on horseback, were a miracle in that part of the country.

Whatever, however, was wanting in the town, was more than made up by the surrounding country, which becomes very beautiful in the immediate environs of Breteuil. For the five or six miles beyond the town, towards Clermont, the scenery is enchanting. The vines, which here commence, were in bloom, the road fringed with orchards, and even the corn-fields hedged round with apple-trees. In the middle of every field was an elm or a chesnut, which by the luxuriance of its foliage seemed planted in other ages. On each side of the road, moreover, at the distance of a mile or a league, were the towers of village churches rising from amidst similar groves, whilst a chateau perhaps crowned the hill, and completed the landscape. Bye-paths, and narrow roads, leading to one or other of these villages, intersected the corn-fields in every direction; and as the corn was full-grown and yellow, and the day beautifully serene, nothing could be more grateful than this prospect. The heart of man seems peculiarly formed to relish the beauties of Nature, and to feel the bounties of Providence. What artificial beauty can equal that of a corn-field? What emotion is so lively, and so fully pervades every feeling, as that excited by the cornucopia of Nature, and the flowery plenty of the approaching harvest?

The same scenery continues with little variation to Clermont, the country improving, and the roads becoming worse. In this interval, however, I passed several chateaux in ruins, and several farms and houses, on which were affixed notices that they were to be let or sold. On inquiring the rent and purchase of one of them, I found it to be so cheap, that could I have reconciled myself to French manners, and promised myself any suitable assistance from French labourers, I should have seriously thought of making a purchase. An estate of eleven hundred acres, seven hundred of which were in culture, the remainder wood and heath, was offered for sale for 8000 Louis. The mansion-house was indeed in ruin beyond the possibility of repair, but the land, under proper cultivation, would have paid twenty-five per cent. on the purchase-money. The main point of such purchases, however, is contained in these words: Under proper cultivation. Nothing is so absurd as the expectation of a foreign purchaser, and particularly of a gentleman, that he will be able to transfer the improved system of cultivation of his own country into a kingdom at least a century behind the former. As far as his own manual labour goes, as far as he will take the plough, the harrow, and the broadcast himself, so far may he procure the execution of his own ideas. But it is in vain to endeavour to infuse this knowledge or this practice into French labourers; you might as well put a pen in the hand of a Hottentot, and expect him to write his name. The ill success of half the foreign purchasers must be imputed to this oversight. An American or an Englishman passes over a French or German farm, and sees land of the most productive powers reduced to sterility by slovenly management. A suggestion immediately arises in his mind—how much might this land be made to produce under a more intelligent cultivation? Full of this idea he perhaps inquires the price, and finding it about one-tenth of what such land would cost in England, immediately makes his purchase, settles, and begins his operations. Here his eyes are soon opened. He must send to England for all his implements; and even then his French labourers neither can or will learn the use of them. An English ploughman becomes necessary; the English ploughman accordingly comes, but shortly becomes miserable amongst French habits and French fellow-labourers.

In this manner have failed innumerable attempts of this kind within my own knowledge. It is impossible to transplant the whole of the system of one country into another. The English or the American farmer may emigrate and settle in France, and bring over his English plough and English habits, but he will still find a French soil, a French climate, French markets, and French labourers. The course of his crops will be disturbed by the necessity of some subservience to the peculiar wants of the country and the demands of the market. He cannot, for example, persevere in his turnips, where he can find no cattle to eat them, no purchasers for his cattle, and where, from the openness of the climate in winter, the crop must necessarily rot before he can consume it. For the same reason, his clover cultivation becomes as useless. To say all in a word, I know not how an English or an American farmer could make a favourable purchase in France, though the French Government should come forward with its protection. The habits of the country have become so accommodated to its agriculture, that they each mutually support the other, and a more improved system can only be introduced in the proportion in which these national habits can be fundamentally changed. But such changes must necessarily be gradual and slow, and must not be reckoned upon by an individual.

I found myself so indisposed at Clermont, that I retired very early to my bed. My complaint was a giddiness in the head, brought on by riding in the sun. Every country has its peculiar medicine as well as its religion, and in every country there are certain family receipts, certain homely prescriptions, which, from their experienced efficacy, merit more attention than a member of the faculty would be inclined to give them. My host at Clermont accordingly became my physician, and by his advice I bathed my feet in warm water, and getting into bed between the blankets, after drinking about a quart of cold spring-water, I can only say that the remedy had its full effect. After a violent perspiration in the night I fell into a sound sleep, and awoke in the morning in such complete health and spirits, as to ride to Chantilly to breakfast.

Throughout the morning's journey, the scenery was very nearly similar to what I had previously passed, except that it was richer and more varied with habitations. The peasantry, moreover, were occupied in the same manner in getting in their hay-harvest, which, from reasons that I cannot comprehend, seemed more backward as I approached to the metropolis. This may partly, indeed, be owing to what will appear a very extraordinary cause—the excellence of the climate. The French farmer can trust the skies; he sees a cloudless sky in the night, and has no fear that its serenity will be shortly disturbed. He is a total stranger to that vicissitude of sunshine, rain, and tempest, which in a moment confounds all the labours of the English husbandmen. The same sun that shines to-day will shine to-morrow. In this happy confidence he stacks his hay in small cocks in the field where it grows, and only carries it away at his leisure. His manner of carrying is as slovenly as all his other management. Annette carries an apron-full, Jeannette an handkerchief-full, and Lubin a barrow-full. Some of it is packed in sheets and blankets. Some of this hay was very bad in quality, and as crops, still worse in quantity. Being too much exposed to the sun, it was little better than so much coarse straw. Being merely thrown together, without being trodden, when carried into the hay-loft, it loses whatever fragrance it may have hitherto retained. I do not think an English horse would eat it.

Chantilly totally disappointed my expectations. The dæmon of anarchy has here raised a superb trophy on a monument of ruins. The principal building has been demolished for the sake of the materials; the stables, and that part of the ancient establishment denominated Le petit Chateau, are all that remain. I was informed by the people of the inn, that the whole had been purchased in the revolutionary period by a petty provincial builder, who had no sooner completed his installments, than he began the demolition of the building, and the cutting down the trees in the grounds. Buonaparte, fortunately for Chantilly, became Chief Consul before the whole was destroyed; Chantilly was then re-purchased, and is now the property of the Government.

The road now began to have some appearance of an approach to the capital of the kingdom. I could not however but still observe, that there were but few carriages compared to what I had seen within a similar distance of London, and even of New York. The several vehicles were mostly constructed in the same manner as vehicles of the same distinction in England. The charette, or cart in common use, was the only exception on the favourable side. This vehicle seemed to me so well adapted to its purpose, as to merit a particular description.

The charette, then, consists principally of two parts—the carriage, and the body. The carriage part is very simple, being composed of two long shafts of wood, about twenty feet in length, connected together by cross bars, so as to form the bed, and on which boards are laid, as the occasion may require. In the same manner the sides, a front, and back, may be added at pleasure. The axle and wheels are in the usual place and form. Upon this carriage is fixed the moveable body, consisting of a similar frame-work of two shafts connected by cross bars. This body moves upon an axletree, and extending some feet beyond the carriage behind, it is let down with ease to receive its load, which the body moving, as before described, on a pivot, or axle, is easily purchased up from before.

Nearly half way between Chantilly and Paris, I passed a handsome chateau to the right, which is now occupied as a school. This establishment was commenced by an Englishman, in the short interval of the peace of Amiens, and he was upon the point of making a rapid fortune, when in common with the other Englishmen at that time in France, he was ordered to Verdun. His school now passed to his French usher, who continuing to conduct it upon the same plan, that is, with the order and intelligence common in every English school, has increased its reputation, and reaps his merited reward by general encouragement. The rate of the boarders at this academy may serve to illustrate the comparative cheapness of every thing in France. The boarders are provided with classic instruction of every kind, as likewise the most eminent masters in all the fine arts, and personal accomplishments, to which is to be added clothes, at forty guineas per annum. An English or American school on the same plan, and conducted in the same style, could not be less than double, if not triple the above-mentioned sum.

I reached Paris at an early hour in the afternoon, and having letters for Mr. Younge, the confidential secretary to Mr. Armstrong, immediately waited upon him, that his information might assist me as to finding suitable apartments. Lodgings in Paris are infinitely more expensive than in London, and with not one-half the comfort. I did not find Mr. Younge at his house; but upon hearing my name, his Lady received me as an expected friend, and relieved me from the necessity of further search, by informing me that Mr. Younge had expected me, and provided apartments for me in his own house. I shall have future occasion to mention, that the beautiful Lady of this Gentleman was a Frenchwoman, and that he had been about six months married to her when I arrived in Paris. She was the niece of the celebrated Lally Tolendal, and had all the elegance, beauty, and dignity which seems characteristic of that family. I never saw a woman, whose perfect beauty excited in me at first sight such a mixed emotion of wonder, awe, and pleasure.

*A Week in Paris—Objects and Occurrences—National Library—A French Route—Fashionable French Supper—Conceits—Presentation at Court—Audience.*

AS my purpose in visiting France was not to see Paris, I resolved to make my stay in this gay capital as short as possible. I entered it on the Tuesday afternoon, and determined to leave it and pursue my journey into the provinces on the following Monday. I had therefore little time to see the singularities of this celebrated metropolis; but I made the best of this time, and had the advantage of Mr. Younge's knowledge and guidance.

There is no place in the world, perhaps, more distinguished for literary eminence, in every part of art and science, than Paris. The literary institutions of Paris, therefore, were the objects of my first visit. Every capital has its theatres, public gardens, and palaces; but Paris alone has its public libraries on a scale of equal utility and magnificence. In Paris alone, science seems to be considered as an object of importance to mankind, and therefore as a suitable object for the protection of Government. In Paris alone, to say all in a word, the poorest student, the most ragged philosopher, has all the treasures of princes at his command; the National Library opens at his call, and the most expensive books are delivered for his use.

On the morning following my arrival, Mr. Younge accompanied me to the National Library. On entering it, we ascended a most superb staircase painted by Pellegrine, by which we were led to the library on the first floor. It consists of a suite of spacious and magnificent apartments, extending round three sides of a quadrangle. The books are ranged around the sides, according to the order of the respective subjects, and are said to amount to nearly half a million. Each division has an attending librarian, of whom every one may require the book he wishes, and which is immediately delivered to him. Being themselves gentlemen, there is no apprehension that they will accept any pecuniary remuneration; but there is likewise a strict order that no money shall be given to any of the inferior attendants. There are tables and chairs in numbers, and nothing seemed neglected, which could conduce even to the comfort of the readers.

The most complete department of the library is that of the manuscripts. This collection amounts to nearly fifty thousand volumes, and amongst them innumerable letters, and even treatises, by the early kings of France. A manuscript is shewn as written by Louis the Fourteenth: it is entitled, "Memoirs of his own Time, written by the King himself." I much doubt, however, the authenticity of this production. Louis the Fourteenth had other more immediate concerns than writing the history of France. France is full of these literary forgeries. Every king of France, if the titles of books may be received as a proof of their authenticity, has not only written his life, but written it like a philosopher and historian, candidly confessing his errors and abusing his ministers.

The second floor of the building contains the genealogies of the French families. They are deposited in boxes, which are labelled with the several family names. They are considered as public records, and are only producible in the courts of justice, in order to determine the titles to real property. No one is allowed to copy them except by the most special permission, which is never granted but to histriographers of established name and reputation. The cabinet of antiques is stated to be very rich, and, to judge by appearances, is not inferior to its reputation. The collection was made by Caylus. It chiefly consists of vases, busts, and articles of domestic use amongst the Romans. The greater part of them have been already copied as models, in the ornamenting of furniture, by the Parisian artists. This fashion indeed is carried almost to a mania. Every thing must be Greek and Roman without any reference to Nature or propriety. For example, what could be so absurd as the natural realization of some of these capricious ornaments? What lady would chose to sleep in a bed, up the pillars of which serpents were crawling? Yet is such realization the only criterion of taste and propriety.

The cabinet of engravings detained us nearly two hours. The portfeuilles containing the prints are distributed into twelve classes. Some of these divisions invited us to a minute inspection. Such was the class containing the French fashions from the age of Clovis to

Louis the Sixteenth. In another class was the costume of every nation in the world; in a third, portraits of eminent persons of all ages and nations; and in a fourth, a collection of prints relating to public festivals, cavalcades, tournaments, coronations, royal funerals, &c. France is the only kingdom in the world which possesses a treasure like this, and which knows how to estimate it at its proper value.

From the National Library we drove to the Athenée, a library and lecture institution, supported by voluntary subscription. It is much of the same nature as an institution of a similar kind in London, termed the British Institute; but the French Athenæum has infinitely the advantage. The subscription is cheaper, being about four Louis annually, and the lectures are more elegant, if not more scientific. There are usually three lectures daily; the first on sciences, and the other two on belles lettres. The lecture on science is considered as very able, but those on the belles lettres were merely suited, as I understood, to French frivolity. The rooms were so full as to render our stay unpleasant, and we thereby lost an anatomy lecture, which was about to commence. I should not forget to mention, that all the Parisian journals and magazines, and many of the German periodical works, were lying on the tables, and the library seemed altogether as complete as it was comfortable. The subscribers are numerous, and the institution itself in fashion. How long it will so last, no one will venture to predict.

The library of the Pantheon and that of the Institute finished our morning's occupation. They are both on the same scale and nearly on the same general plan as the National Library. The library of the Institute, however, is only open to foreigners and the members of the Institute. The Institute holds its sitting every month, and, according to all report, is then frivolous enough. I had not an opportunity of being present at one of these sittings, but from what I heard, I did not much regret my disappointment.

We returned home to dress for dinner. Mr. Younge informed, me, that he expected a very large party in the evening, chiefly French, and as his lady herself was a French woman, and had arranged her domestic establishment accordingly, I felt some curiosity.

About eight, or nearer nine, Mr. Younge and myself, with two or three other of the dinner company, were summoned up to the drawing-room. The summons itself had something peculiar. The doors of the parlour, which were folding, were thrown open, and two female attendants, dressed like vestals, and holding torches of white wax, summoned us by a low curtsey, and preceded us up the great staircase to the doors of the anti-chamber, where they made another salutation, and took their station on each side. The anti-chamber was filled with servants, who were seated on benches fixed to the wall, but who did not rise on our entry. Some of them were even playing at cards, others at dominos, and all of them seemed perfectly at their ease. The anti-chamber opened by an arched door-way into an handsome room, lighted by a chandelier of the most brilliant cut glass; the pannels of the room were very tastily painted, and the glasses on each side very large, and in magnificent frames. The further extremity of this room opened by folding doors into the principal drawing-room, where the company were collected. It was brilliantly lighted, as well by patent lamps, as by a chandelier in the middle. The furniture had a resemblance to what I had seen in fashionable houses in England. The carpet was of red baize with a Turkish border, and figured in the middle like an harlequin's jacket. The principal novelty was a blue ribbon which divided the room lengthways, the one side of it being for the dancers, the other for the card-players. The ribbon was supported at proper distances by white staves, similar to those of the court ushers.

The ball had little to distinguish it from the balls of England and America, except that the ladies danced with infinitely more skill, and therefore with more grace. The fashionable French dancing is exactly that of our operas. They are all figurantes, and care not what they exhibit, so as they exhibit their skill. I could not but figure to myself the confusion of an English girl, were she even present at a French assembly. Yet so powerful is habit, that not only did the ladies seem insensible, but even the gentlemen, such as did not dance, regarded them with indifference.

Cotillons and waltzes were the only dances of the evening. The waltzes were danced in couples, twenty or thirty at a time. The measure was quick, and all the parties seemed animated. I cannot say that I saw any thing indecorous in the embraces of the ladies and their partners, except in the mere act itself; but the waltz will never become a current fashion in England or America.

There is no precedency in a French assembly except amongst the Military. This is managed with much delicacy. Every group is thrown as much as possible into a circle. The tables are all circular, and cotillons are chiefly preferred from having this quality.

I did not join the card-players; there were about half a dozen tables, and the several parties appeared to play very high. When the game, or a certain number of games were over, the parties rose from their seats, and bowing to any whom they saw near them, invited them to succeed them in their seats. These invitations were sometimes accepted, but more frequently declined. The division of the drawing-room set apart for the card-players served rather as a promenade for the company who did not dance; they here ranged themselves in a line along the ribbon, and criticised the several dancers. Some of these spectators seemed most egregious fops. One of them, with the exception of his linen, was dressed completely in purple silk or satin, and another in a rose-coloured silk coat, with white satin waistcoat and small clothes, and white silk stockings. The greater part of the ladies were dressed in fancy habits from the antique. Some were sphinxes, some vestals, some Dians, half a dozen Minervas, and a score of Junos and Cleopatras. One girl was pointed out to me as being perfectly á l'Anglaise. Her hair, perfectly undressed, was combed off her forehead, and hung down her back in its full length behind. She reminded me only of a school-boy playing without his hat.

We were summoned to the supper table about three in the morning. This repast was a perfect English dinner. Soup, fish, poultry and ragouts, succeeded each other in almost endless variety. A fruit-basket was served round by the servants together with the bread-basket, and a small case of liqueurs was placed at every third plate. Some of these were contained in glass figures of Cupids, in which case, in order to get at the liqueur, it was necessary to break off a small globule affixed to the breast of the figure. The French confectioners are more ingenious than delicate in these contrivances; but the French ladies seem better pleased with such conceit in proportion to their intelligible references. Some of these naked Cupids, which were perfect in all their parts, were handed from the gentlemen to the ladies, and from the ladies to each other, and as freely examined and criticised, as if they had been paintings of birds. The gentlemen, upon their parts, were equally as facetious upon the naked Venuses; and a Swan affixed to a Leda, was the lucky source of innumerable pleasant questions and answers. Every thing, in a word, is tolerated which can in any way be passed into an equivoque. Their conversation in this respect resembles their dress—no matter how thin that covering may be, so that there be one.

So much for a French assembly or fashionable rout, which certainly excells an English one in elegance and fancy, as much as it falls short of it in substantial mirth. The French, it must be confessed, infinitely excell every other nation in all things connected with spectacle, and more or less this spectacle pervades all their parties. They dance, they converse, they sing, for exhibition, and as if they were on the stage. Their conversation, therefore, has frequently more wit than interest, and their dancing more vanity than mirth. They seem in both respects to want that happy carelessness which pleases by being pleased. A Frenchwoman is a figurante even in her chit-chat.

It may be expected that I did not omit to visit the theatres. Mr. Younge accompanied me successively to nearly all of them—two or three in an evening. Upon this subject, however, I shall say nothing, as every book of travels has so fully described some or other of them, that nothing in fact is further required.

I had resolved not to leave Paris without seeing the Emperor, and being informed that he was to hold an audience on the following day, I applied to Mr. Younge to procure my formal introduction. With this purpose we waited upon General Armstrong, who sent my name to the Grand Chamberlain with the necessary formalities. This formality is a certificate under the hand of the Ambassador; that the person soliciting the introduction has been introduced at his own Court, or that, according to the best knowledge of the Ambassador, he is not a Merchant—a *Negociant actuel*. It may be briefly observed, however, that the French Negotiant answers better to the English Mechanic, than to the honorable appellation, Merchant.—General Armstrong promised me a very interesting spectacle in the

Imperial audience. "It's the most splendid Court in Europe," said he: "the Court of London, and even of Vienna, will not bear a comparison with it." Every one agreed in the justice of this remark, and my curiosity was strongly excited.

On the appointed day, about three o'clock, Mr. Younge accompanied me to the Palace, where we were immediately conducted to a splendid saloon, which is termed the Ambassadors' hall. Refreshments were here handed round to the company, which was very numerous, and amongst them many German Princes in their grand court dress. The conversation became very general; those who had seen Bonaparte describing him to those who were about to be introduced. Every one agreed that he was the most extraordinary man that Europe had produced in many centuries, and that even his appearance was in no slight degree indicative of his character. "He possesses an eye," said one gentleman, "in which Lavater might have understood an hero." Mr. Younge confirmed this observation, and prepared me to regard him with more than common attention.

The doors of the saloon were at length thrown open, and some of the officers of the Grand Chamberlain, with white wands and embroidered robes and scarfs, bowing low to the company, invited us, by waving their staves, to follow them up the grand staircase. Every one now arranged themselves, in pairs, behind their respective Ambassadors, and followed the ushers in procession, according to the precedence of their respective countries, the Imperial, Spanish, and Neapolitan Ambassadors forming the van. The staircase was lined on both sides with grenadiers of the Legion of Honour, most of whom, privates as well as officers, were arrayed in the order. The officers, as we passed, exchanged salutes with the Ambassadors; and as the Imperial Ambassador, who led the procession, reached the door of the anti-chamber, two trumpeters on each side played a congratulatory flourish. The ushers who had led us so far, now took their stations on each side the door, and others, in more splendid habits, succeeded them in the office of conducting us.

We now entered the anti-chamber, in which was stationed the regular guard of the palace. We were here saluted both by privates and officers, the Imperial Guard being considered as part of the household. From the anti-chamber we passed onwards through nearly a dozen most splendid apartments, and at length reached the presence-chamber.

My eyes were instantly in search of the Emperor, who was at the farther extremity, surrounded by a numerous circle of officers and counsellors. The circle opened on our arrival, and withdrew behind the Emperor. The whole of our company now ranged themselves, the Ambassadors in front, and their several countrymen behind their respective Ministers.

Bonaparte now advanced to the Imperial Ambassador, with whom, when present, he always begins the audience. I had now an opportunity to regard him attentively. His person is below the middle size, but well composed; his features regular, but in their *tout ensemble* stern and commanding; his complexion sallow, and his general mien military. He was dressed very splendidly in purple velvet, the coat and waistcoat embroidered with gold bees, and with the grand star of the Legion of Honour worked into the coat.

He passed no one without notice, and to all the Ambassadors he spoke once or twice. When he reached General Armstrong, he asked him, whether America could not live, without foreign commerce as well as France? and then added, without waiting for his answer, "There is one nation in the world which must be taught by experience, that her Merchants are not necessary to the existence of all other nations, and that she cannot hold us all in commercial slavery: England is only sensible in her compters."

The audience took up little less than two hours, after which the Emperor withdrew into an adjoining apartment; and the company departed in the same order, and with the same appendages, as upon their entrance.

### CHAP. X.

*Departure from Paris for the Loire—Breakfast at Palaiseau—A Peasant's Wife—Rambouillet—Magnificent Chateau—French Curé—Chartres—Difference of Old French and English Towns—Subterraneous Church—Curious Preservation of the Dead—Angers—Arrival at Nantes.*

ON my first arrival at Paris, I had intended to remain there only till the following week; but the kind importunities of Mr. Younge and his family, induced me to consent to prolong my stay for some days, and an arrangement was at length made, which caused me most cheerfully to protract it still further. This arrangement was, that if I would remain in Paris till after the National Fêtes, Mr. Younge, his lady, and her niece, Mademoiselle St. Sillery, would form a travelling party, and accompany me in my tour along the banks of the Loire, and thence along the Southern Coast. As I had no other purpose but to see France, its scenery and its manners, nothing could possibly have fallen out more correspondent with my wishes. I shall here cursorily mention, that Mademoiselle St. Sillery, with the single exception of her aunt, was the handsomest woman I had yet seen in France.

If I pass over the National Fêtes, it is because they differed nothing from those which preceded them, and which have been minutely detailed by every Traveller who has written his Tour. These national spectacles have nothing in them which rewards the trouble of pressing through the mob to see them. It consisted of nothing but a succession of buffooneries and fire-works. The fire-works were magnificent—all the other sports contemptible. In a word, I was so anxious to leave Paris, and to get into the woods and fields, that the bustle around me scarcely attracted my attention.

At length, the morning of the 28th of July arrived, and after all due preparations, I had the long wished-for pleasure of seeing Mr. Younge's coach at the door, with its travelling appendages. Mr. Younge preferring to accompany me on horseback, the coach was left to the ladies. In this manner we left Paris at six o'clock on a lovely summer's morning, and in less than half an hour were three miles on the road to Chartres, which we hoped to reach to sleep.

I had again occasion to observe, how much the environs of Paris differed from those of London. Scarcely had we reached our first stage (about seven miles), before every appendage of a metropolitan city had disappeared. With the single exception of the road, which still continued worthy of a great nation, the scenery and objects were as retired as in the most remote corner of England. This absence of commercial traffic has, however, one advantage—it adds much to the beauty and romance of the country. In England, the manners, habits, and dress of the capital, pervade to the remotest angle of the kingdom: there is little variety in passing from London to Penzance. On the other hand, in France, every Province has still its characteristic dress and manners; and you get but a few miles from Paris, before you find yourself amongst a new order of beings.

We breakfasted at Palaiseau, a beautiful village, about twelve miles from Paris. The inn being dirty, and having no appearance of being in a situation to accommodate us to our wishes, Mr. Younge ordered the coach to drive to a small cottage at the further end of the village. Our party here dismounted; a small trunk, containing a breakfast equipage, was taken from the coach, and the table was covered in an instant. The woman of the house had been a servant of Mrs. Younge's, and married from the family; her husband was a petty farmer, and was out in his fields. Nothing could persuade Susette to sit in the presence of our ladies; but she was talkative in the extreme, and seemed to be much attached to Mrs. Younge, playing as it were with her hair as she waited behind her chair. To Mr. Younge's questions, whether she was happy, and how she liked her new state, she replied very carelessly, that her husband was as good as husbands usually are; that, indeed, he had an affair with another woman; but that he was gay, and not jealous, and therefore that she overlooked it. Whilst she was saying this, the latch of the door was raised, and a sturdy young peasant made his appearance; but seeing an unexpected company, drew back in some confusion. Mr. Younge cast a significant look at the ladies and Susette, whose looks explained that they were not without foundation. Such are the morals, or rather the manners, of the lower order of French wives. Gallantry is, in fact, as much in fashion, and as generally prevalent through all orders, as in the most corrupt æra of the monarchy—perhaps, indeed, more so; as religion, though manifestly reviving, has not yet recovered its former vigour.

Having remounted our horses, and the ladies re-ascended into their coach, we continued our journey through a country continually changing. My observations on the road, undeceived me in a point of some importance. I had hitherto believed France to have been an open country, almost totally without enclosures, except the pales and ditches necessary to distinguish properties. This opinion had been confirmed by the appearances of the road from Calais to Paris. It was now, however, totally done away, as the country on each side of me was as thickly enclosed, as any of the most cultivated counties in England. Hereafter, let no traveller assert that France is a country of open fields; three-fourths of the kingdom is enclosed, even to the most minute divisions. The enclosures, indeed, have not the neatness of those of England; the hedges are rough and open, and there are few gates, and no stiles. The French farmers, however, have already began to adopt much of the English system in the management of their farms. According to the information of Mr. Younge, many of the emigrés having returned to France, have given some valuable instructions to the people in these important points; France is accordingly much better cultivated than hitherto.

Mr. Younge had the politeness to answer my questions respecting the country through which we were passing, in the utmost possible detail; and as he himself had traversed France in all directions, and was not without some purpose of future settlement, his information was accurate and valuable. He gave me to understand that, with the single exception of the good enclosures, nothing could be so miserable as the system of agriculture along the whole road from Paris to Mans. The general quality of the soil is light and sandy, and exactly suited to the English system of alternate crops of corn and roots; yet on such a soil, the common course is no other than, fallow, wheat, barley, for nine years successively; after which the land is pared and burnt, and then suffered to be a fallow in weeds for another year, when the same course is recommenced. "Under such management," continued Mr. Younge, "you will not be surprised that the average produce of the province of Bretagne does not exceed twelve bushels of wheat, and eighteen of barley. Turnips they have no idea of; and as the proportion of cattle is very small, the land is necessarily still farther impoverished from want of manure. The rents are about 18 livres, or 15s. English; the price in purchase from 15l to 18l English. The size of the farms is generally about 80 acres English; they are usually held from year to year, but there are some leases. Having got rid of tithes, and the taxes being very moderate," said Mr. Younge, "the price of land in France, both as to rent or purchase, is certainly very moderate; and if we could but import English or American workmen, or bring the French labourers to English or American habits, no good farmer would hesitate a moment as to settlement in France. But the French labourers are obstinate in proportion to their ignorance, and without exception are the most ignorant workmen in the world. Nothing is to be done with them; and though the Emperor has issued a decree, by which foreigners settling with a view to agriculture or manufactures, and giving security that they will not leave the kingdom, may become denizens, I must still hesitate as to recommending a foreigner to seek a French naturalization."

In this conversation, after a long but not wearisome journey, we reached Rambouillet. The trunk was again brought from the coach, and a table furnished with knives, spoons, and clean linen—a kind of essentials seldom to be seen in a French inn, and more particularly in such inns as we had reason to expect at some of our stages, in the course of our long tour. A servant had likewise been sent before, so that a tolerable dinner was already in a state of preparation. Being informed, however, that we had an hour still good, Mr. Younge and Mademoiselle St. Sillery insisted upon taking me to see the celebrated chateau in which Francis the First, breathed his last.

Nothing can be more miserable, nothing more calculated to inspire melancholy, than the situation and approach to this immense and most disproportioned building. It is situated in a park, in the midst of woods and waters, and most unaccountably, the very lowest ground in a park of two thousand acres is chosen for its site. The approach to it from the village is by a long avenue, planted on both sides by double and treble rows of lofty trees, the tops of which are so broad and thick as almost to meet each other. This avenue opens into a lawn, in the centre of which is the chateau. It is an heavy and vast structure, entirely of brick, and with the turrets, arches, and corners, characteristic of the Gothic order. The property of it belongs at present to the Nation, that is to say, it was not sold amongst the other, confiscated estates; something of an Imperial establishment, therefore, is resident in the chateau, consisting of a company of soldiers, with two officers, and an housekeeper. One of the officers had the politeness to become our guide, and to lead us from room to room, explaining as he went whatever seemed to excite our attention.

31

Louis the Fourteenth held his court in this castle for some years; and from respect to his memory, the apartment in which he slept and held his levee, is still retained in the same condition in which it was left by that Monarch. This chamber is a room nearly thirty yards in length by eighteen in width, and lofty in proportion: the windows like those of a church. On the further extremity is a raised floor, where stands the royal bed of purple velvet and gold, lined with white satin painted in a very superior style. The colours, both of the painting and the velvet, still remain; and two pieces of coarse linen are shewed as the royal sheets. The counterpane is of red velvet, embroidered as it were with white lace, and with a deep gold fringe round the edges: this is likewise lined with white satin, and marked at the corners with a crown and fleur de lys. On each side of the bed are the portraits of Louis the Fourteenth and Fifteenth, of Philip the Fourth of Spain, and of his Queen. The portrait of Louis the Fourteenth more peculiarly attracted my attention, having been mentioned by several historians to be the best existing likeness of that celebrated Monarch. If Louis resembled his picture, he was much handsomer than he is described to have been by the memoir-writers of his age: his countenance has an air of much haughtiness and self-confidence, but without any mixture of ill-humour. The chief peculiarity in his habit was a deep lace ruff, and a doublet of light blue, very nearly resembling the jacket of the English light cavalry. This portrait was taken when the King was in his twenty-eighth year, and therefore is probably a far more correct resemblance than those which were taken at a more advanced period—so true is the assertion, of the poet, that old men are all alike.

Immediately over that line of the apartment where the raised floor terminates, is a gilded rod extending along the ceiling. When the King held his court at Rambouillet, a curtain only separated his chamber and the levee-room. In the latter room are several portraits of the Peers of France during the reign of Louis the Fifteenth, with those of some Spanish Grandees.

We visited several other rooms, all of them magnificently furnished, and all the furniture apparently of the same æra. The grand saloon appeared to me to be the largest room I had ever seen; the floor is of white marble, as are likewise two ranges of Corinthian pillars on each side of the apartment. Its height, however, is not proportioned to its length, a defect which, added to its narrowness, gives it the air of a gallery rather than of a banquetting-room.

We had not time enough to walk over the gardens; but, from a cursory view of them, did not much regret our loss. They appeared spacious enough; but so divided and intersected into plots, borders, narrow and broad walks, terraces, and flowerbeds in the shape of stars, as to resemble any thing but what would be called a garden in England and America. This style of gardening was introduced into France by Le Notre, and some centuries must yet pass away before the French gardeners will acquire a more correct taste. What would not English taste have effected with the capabilities of Rambouillet? A park of two thousand acres in front, and a forest of nearly thirty thousand behind—all this, in the hands of Frenchmen, is thrown away; the park is but a meadow, and the forest a neglected wood.

Upon our return to dinner, we found the *Curé* of the village in rapid conversation with Madame. The appearance of our equipage, consisting of four horses in the coach, and three riding horses, had attracted him to the inn; and Madame, having seen him, had invited him to join us at dinner. He was a pleasant little man, and related to us many traditional anecdotes of Louis the Fourteenth. This King was notoriously one of the most gallant of the race of Capet. "Whilst resident at Rambouillet," said the Curé, "being one day hunting, and separated from his suite, he fell in with two young girls, the daughters of the better kind of French farmers. The girls were nutting in the forest, and perfectly strangers to the King's person. Louis entered into conversation with them, and—"

The good Curé's narrative was here interrupted by dinner, much to the disappointment of Mademoiselle St. Sillery, who entreated him to resume his narrative upon the disappearance of the first dish. "I should think, Angela," said Mrs. Younge, "that Monsieur Curé would continue it to more advantage in the coach. The gentleman has informed me," continued she, addressing herself to Mr. Younge, "that he has some business at Chartres; and thinking it would add much to our general pleasure, I have invited him to take the spare seat in our carriage." Mr. Younge could do no less than second this invitation, and our party was thus reinforced by the addition of a little gossiping French Curé.

Monsieur Guygny, the name of this gentleman, was not however so much a Curé, as to be deficient in gallantry to the ladies, and Mademoiselle St. Sillery, as I thought, seemed to consider him as a valuable acquisition to our travelling suite; she re-ascended the coach with increased spirit, and the good Curé followed with true French agility. Thus is it with French manners. Upon inquiry from Mr. Younge I learnt, that not one of the party had ever seen or heard of Monsieur Guygny before they had now met at Rambouillet.

I felt some curiosity as to the interrupted narrative, even in despite of the evident frivolity of the narrator. The arrangement of the party in the coach compelled me to hear it at second hand, and I found it less frivolous than I had anticipated: it was an amour between the King and a peasant's daughter, in which the King conducted himself in a manner as little excusable in a monarch, as in a more humble individual. The amour was at length discovered by the pregnancy of the unfortunate girl, who believed herself married to the King in the character of an officer of his suite, and who, upon discovering the deception, died of shame and grief. Her tomb is said to be still extant, and to be distinguished by a fleur de lys impressed on it by command of the King. The story is said to be well founded: be this as it may, our ladies seemed to have received it as gospel.

We reached Chartres by sunset. Nothing could be more delightful than the approach to the town, which is situated upon the knoll of an hill, the houses intermixed with trees, and the setting sun gilding the spires of the churches and convent. The town is divided into two parts by a small river; the further part was situated upon the ascent, the other part upon the banks of the river. On each side of the town are hills, covered with woods, from the midst of which were visible the gilded spires of convents and churches, whilst the intervening plains were covered with corn-fields. The peasantry, as we passed them, seemed clean, well-fed, and happy; we saw several groups of them enjoying themselves in the evening dance. Our carriage was overtaken by them more than once; they presented flowers and fruits to our ladies, and refused any return. Some of the younger women, though sun-burnt, were handsome; and many of them, from their fanciful dresses, resembled the cottagers as exhibited on the stage. The men, on the other hand, were a most ugly race of beings, diminutive in size, and with the features of an old baboon. Mr. Younge, indeed, in some degree accounted for this, by the information that the best men had been taken for the armies.

Having taken our tea, and seen the necessary preparation for our beds, our ladies changed their dresses, and, attended by the Curé, sallied forth to the evening promenade still customary in all the French towns. Mr. Younge and myself availed ourselves of this opportunity to visit the curiosities of the town.

I have frequently had occasion to remark, that the old French towns have a very prominent distinction. The inland towns of England, be their antiquity what it may, retain but little of their ancient form; from the necessary effects of a brisk trade, the several houses have so often changed owners, and the owners have usually been so substantial in their circumstances, that there is scarcely a house, perhaps, but what in twenty years has been rebuilt from its fundamental stone. It is not the same with the houses in the old towns of France. A French tradesman's house is like his stocking—he never thinks that he wants a new one, as long as he can in any way darn his old one; he never thinks of building a new wall, as long as he can patch his old one; he repairs his house piece-meal as it falls down: the repairs, therefore, are always made so as to match the breach. In this manner the original form of the house is preserved for some centuries, and, as philosophers say of the human body, retains its identity, though every atom of it may have been changed.

It is thus with Chartres, one of the most ancient towns in France, which in every house bears evident proofs of its antiquity, the streets being in straight lines, and the houses dark, large, but full of small rooms. The town, as I have before said, is divided into two parts, by the river Eure, and thence, according to the French historians, was called *Autricum* by the Romans. It is surrounded by a wall, and has nine gates, the greater part of them of stone, and of a very ancient architecture; they are all surmounted by a figure of the Holy Virgin, the former patroness of the city. The cathedral church, if the traditional accounts may be believed, was formerly a temple of the Druids, dedicated to the *Virgo Paritura*; and though this antiquity may be fairly disputed, the structure is evidently of the most remote ages. According to the actual records, it was burnt by lightning in the year of our Lord 1020, and was then rebuilt upon its ancient foundations, and according to its former form, by Fulbert, at that time the Bishop. It is thus, in every respect, the most ancient monument in France, and is well deserving of being visited by travellers. We were lost in astonishment as we descended from the upper church into a subterraneous one, extending under the whole space of the one above it, and having corresponding walls, choir, and even stalls. The bishops, chapter, and principal persons of the city, are here buried.

From the cathedral church, we were conducted to the other curiosities of the city, one of which is well worthy of mention. This is a cave or vault in the parish church of St. André. Upon descending it, our guide removed successively the covers of six coffins, and desired us to examine the bodies. They consisted of four men and two women; the faces, arms, and breasts were naked, and had all the freshness as if dead only the preceding day. One of the men had the mark of a wound under his left breast; it seemed as if made by a pointed sword or pike, and was florid, red, and fresh. "These persons," said our guide, "as you may see by the inscriptions, have been buried from fifty to an hundred years; the wounded man was the Mayor of the town about sixty years since, and was wounded in an affray, of which wound he died." Upon receiving this information, I had the curiosity to examine the vault more accurately: it was walled all around, paved with stones closely cemented, and was evidently more than commonly dry.

We remained at Chartres the whole of the following day; and on the morning of the next, still accompanied by the Curé, continued our journey to Le Mans, where we likewise remained a day, and thence proceeded for Angers. As our projected Tour along the Loire was to commence at Nantes, we were eager to gain that city, and indeed scarcely made use of our eyes, however invited, till we reached it.

Mr. Younge and myself had an hour's walk over Angers; but as we saw it more in detail as we descended the Loire, in the progress of our future Tour, I shall say nothing of it in this place.

Throughout the greater part of this road, as well as of that from Angers to Nantes, nothing could be more delightful than the scenery on both sides, and nothing better than the roads. From La Fleche to Angers, and thence to Ancennis, the country is a complete garden. The hills were covered with vines; every wood had its chateau, and every village its church. The peasantry were clean and happy, the children cheerful and healthy-looking, and the greater part of the younger women spirited and handsome. There was a great plenty of fruit; and as we passed through the villages, it was invariably brought to us, and almost as invariably any pecuniary return refused with a retreating curtsey. One sweet girl, a young peasant, with eyes and complexion which would be esteemed handsome even in Philadelphia, having made Mr. Younge and myself an offering of this kind, replied very prettily to our offer of money, that the women of La Fleche never sold either grapes or water; as much as to say, that the one was as plentiful as the other. Some of these young girls were dressed not only neatly, but tastily. Straw hats are the manufacture of the province; few of them, therefore, but had a straw bonnet, and few of these bonnets were without ribbons or flowers.

We were most unexpectedly detained at Chantoce by an accident to our coach, which was three days before it was repaired. We the less, however, regretted our disappointment, as it rained incessantly, with thunder and lightning, throughout the whole of this time. The weather having cleared, our coach being repaired, and our spirits being renovated by the increased elasticity of the air, the preceding heat having been almost intolerable, we resumed our progress, and at length reached Nantes on or about the evening of the 1st of August.

## CHAP. XI.

*Nantes—Beautiful Situation—Analogy of Architecture with the Character of its Age—Singular Vow of Francis the Second—Departure from Nantes—Country between Nantes and Angers—Angers.*

THE plan of our Tour was, to descend the Loire from Nantes, and thence traversing its banks through nearly two-thirds of its course, cross it by La Charité, and continue our journey in the first place for Languedoc, and thence across that delightful province into Provence, and along the shores of the Mediterranean. Chance in some degree varied our original design; but it will be seen in the sequel, that we executed more of it than we had any reason to anticipate. A traveller in France cannot reckon upon either his road, or his arrival, with as much certainty as in England. Some of the cross roads are absolutely impassable; and the French gentry of late have become so fond of jaunts of pleasure, that if a travelling family should visit them in passing, they will have great difficulty to get away without some addition to their party, and some consequent variation from their projected road.

We remained at Nantes three days, during which time I had leisure enough to visit the town and the neighbourhood.

Nantes is one of the most ancient cities in France; it is the *Condivunum* of the Romans, and the *Civitas Namnetum* of Cæsar. It is mentioned by several Latin writers as a town of moat considerable population under the Roman prefects; and there is every appearance, in several parts of the city, that it has declined much from its original importance. It is still, however, in every respect, a noble city, and, unlike most commercial cities, is as beautifully as it is advantageously situated. It is built on the ascent and summit of an hill, at the foot of which is the Loire, almost as broad, and ten times more beautiful, than the Thames. In the middle of the stream, opposite the town, are several islets, on which are houses and gardens, and which, as seen by the setting sun, about which time there are dancing parties, and marquees ornamented with ribbons, have a most pleasing effect. The town, however, has one defect, which the French want the art or the industry to remove: the Loire is so very shallow near the town, that vessels of any magnitude are obliged to unload at some miles above it. This is a commercial inconvenience, which is not compensated by one of the finest quays in Europe, extending nearly a mile in length, and covered with buildings almost approaching to palaces. If Spain, as the proverb says, have bridges where there is no water, I have seen repeated instances in France where there are quays without trade. This is not, however, the case with Nantes: it has still a brisk interior commerce, and the number of new houses are sufficient proofs that its inhabitants increase in opulence.

Nantes was the residence and the burying place of the ancient Dukes of Bretagne; in the town and neighbourhood, therefore, are many of the relics of these early sovereigns. On an hill to the eastward is the castle in which these princes used to hold their court: it is still entire, though built nearly nine hundred years ago; and the repairs having been made in the character of the original structure, it remains a most perfect specimen of the architecture of the age in which it was built. One room, the hall or banquetting-room, as in all Gothic castles, is of an immense size, and lofty in proportion. The ornaments likewise partake of the character of the age; they are chiefly carved angels, croziers, and other sacred appendages. A remark here struck me very forcibly, that many curious conclusions as to the characters, manners, and even of the detail of domestic economy of men in the early ages, might be deduced from the remains of their architecture. I have read very curious and detailed histories founded only on the figures on medals; the early history of Greece, and that of the lower empire of Rome, have scarcely a better foundation. Now, why may not the same use be made of architecture? Is not the religion of our ancestors legible in the very ornaments of their house? Are not their excessive ignorance and credulity equally visible in the griffins, sphinxes, dragons, mermaids, and chimeras, which are so frequently carved in Gothic roofs, and which are so absurdly mistaken for angels and devils? The analogy might be extended much farther.

The monument of Francis the Second, Duke of Bretagne, and father to Anne of Bretagne, the Queen of France, is one of the most magnificent of the kind in France, and from this circumstance, I suppose, has been suffered to survive the Revolution undefaced. This monument was the work of Michael Colomb, and is one of those works of art which, like the Apollo Belvidere, is sufficient of itself to immortalize its artist. The figures are a curious mixture of the wives and children of the deceased Duke, with angels, cherubs, &c.; but this was the taste of the age, and must not be imputed to Michael Colomb. The heart of Anne is likewise buried in a silver urn in the same vault. The inscription on the tomb relates a vow made by Francis to the Holy Virgin, that if he should obtain a child by his second marriage, he would dedicate a golden image to the Virgin. The prince obtained the child, and the image was made and dedicated.

It would be an injustice, in this account of Nantes, not to mention the inn called the Hotel of Henry the Fourth. It is one of the largest and most magnificently furnished in Europe. It makes up 60 beds, and can take in 100 horses, and an equal proportion of servants. The rooms are let very cheap, considering their quality: two neat rooms may be had for four shillings a day; and a traveller may live very comfortably in the house, and be provided with every thing, for about two guineas per week. Horses are charged at the rate of two shillings only for a day and night. And one thing which ought not to be forgotten, the beds are made, and ladies are attended, by female servants, all of whom are neat, and many of them very pretty girls. The contrary practice, which is almost universal in France, is one of the most unpleasant circumstances to a man educated in old English habits; for my own part, I never could divest myself of my first disgust, at the sight of a huge, bearded, raw-boned fellow, having access to the chamber at all hours, and making the beds, and removing any of the usual appendages of a chamber, in the presence of the ladies.

Having seen enough of Nantes, and exchanged our coach for a kind of open barouche, particularly adapted for the French cross roads, being very narrow, and composed entirely of cane, with removable wheels, so as to take to pieces in an instant, we resumed the line of our Tour, and took the road along the Loire for Ancennis.

It was a beautiful morning, and there being a fair at Mauves, a village on the road, nothing could be more gay than our journey at its commencement. I have forgotten to mention, that Mr. Younge and myself, at the proposal of the ladies, had sent our horses forwards, and therefore had taken our seats in the landau. The conversation of the ladies was so pleasing and so intelligent, that hereafter I adopted this proposal as often as it was offered, and as seldom as possible had recourse to my horse.

Mauves, which was our first stage, is most romantically situated on a hill, which forms one of the banks of the Loire. The country about it, in the richness of its woods, and the verdure of its meadows, most strongly reminded me of England; but I know of no scenery in England, which together with this richness and variety of woodland and meadow, has such a beautiful river as the Loire to complete it in all the qualities of landscape. On each side of this river, from Nantes, are hills, which are wooded to the summit, and there are very few of these wood-tufted hills, which have not their castle or ruined tower. In some of these ancient buildings, there was scarcely any thing remaining but the two towers which guarded the grand portal; but others, being more durably constructed, were still habitable, though still retaining their ancient forms. I have frequently had occasion to observe, that the French gentry, in making their repairs, invariably follow the style of the building; whether through natural taste, or because they repair by piece-meal, and therefore do only what is wanted, I know not. But there is one necessary consequence from this practice, which is, that the remains of antiquity are more perfect in France than in any other kingdom in Europe. From Mauves to Oudon, where we dined, the country is still very thickly wooded and inclosed; the properties evidently very small, and therefore innumerable cottages and small gardens. These cottages usually consist of only one floor, divided into two rooms, and a shed behind. They were generally situated in orchards, and fronted the Loire. They had invariably one or two large trees, which are decorated with ribbons at sunset, as the signal for the dance, which is invariably observed in this part of France. Some of the peasant girls, which came out to us with fruit, were very handsome, though brown. The children, which were in great numbers, looked healthy, but were very scantily clad. None of them had more than a shift and a petticoat, and some of them girls of ten or twelve years of age, only a shift, tied round the waist by a coloured girdle. As seen at some distance, they reminded me very forcibly of the figures in landscape pictures.

We remained at Oudon till near sunset, when we resumed our road to Ancennis, where we intended to sleep. As this was only a distance of seven miles, we took it very leisurely, sometimes riding, and sometimes walking. The evening was as beautiful as is usual in the southern parts of Europe at this season of the year. The road was most romantically recluse, and so serpentine as never to be visible beyond an hundred yards. The nightingales were singing in the adjoining woods. The road, moreover, was bordered on each side by lofty hedges, intermingled with fruit-trees, and even vines in full bearing. At every half mile, a cross road, branching from the main one, led into the recesses of the country, or to some castle or villa on the high grounds which overlook the river. At some of these bye-ways were very curious inscriptions, painted on narrow boards affixed to a tree. Such were, "The way to 'My Heart's Content' is half a league up this road, and then turn to the right, and keep on till you reach it." And another: "The way to 'Love's Hermitage' is up this lane, till you come to the cherry-tree by the side of a chalk-pit, where there is another direction." Mademoiselle Sillery informed me, that these kind of inscriptions were characteristic of the banks of the Loire. "The inhabitants along the whole of the course of this river," said she, "have the reputation, from time immemorial, of being all native poets; and the reputation, like some prophecies, has perhaps been the means of realizing itself. You do not perhaps know, that the Loire is called in the provinces the River of Love; and doubtless its beautiful banks, its green meadows, and its woody recesses, have what the musicians would call a symphony of tone with that passion." I have translated this sentence verbally from my note-book, as it may give some idea of Mademoiselle Sillery. If ever figure was formed to inspire the passion of which she spoke, it was this lady. Many days and years must pass over before I forget our walk on the green road from Oudon to Ancennis—one of the sweetest, softest scenes in France.

We entered the forest of Ancennis as the sun was setting. This forest is celebrated in every ancient French ballad, as being the haunt of fairies, and the scene of the ancient archery of the provinces of Bretagne and Anjou. The road through it was over a green turf, in which the marks of a wheel were scarcely visible The forest on each side was very thick. At short intervals, narrow footpaths struck into the wood. Our carriage had been sent before to Ancennis, and we were walking merrily on, when the well-known sound of the French horn arrested our steps and attention. Mademoiselle Sillery immediately guessed it to proceed from a company of archers; and in a few moments her conjecture was verified by the appearance of two ladies and a gentleman, who issued from one of the narrow paths. The ladies, who were merely running from the gentleman, were very tastily habited in the favourite French dress after the Dian of David; whilst the blue silk jacket and hunting cap of the gentleman gave him the appearance of a groom about to ride a race. Our appearance necessarily took their attention; and after an exchange of salutes, but in which no names were mentioned on either side, they invited us to accompany them to their party, who were refreshing themselves in an adjoining dell. "We have had a party at archery," said one of them, "and Madame St. Amande has won the silver bugle and bow. The party is now at supper, after which we go to the chateau to dance. Perhaps you will not suffer us to repent having met you by refusing to accompany us." Mademoiselle Sillery was very eager to accept this invitation, and looked rather blank when Mrs. Younge declined it, as she wished to proceed on her road as quickly as possible. "You will at least accompany us, merely to see the party."—"By all means," said Mademoiselle Sillery. "I must really regret that I cannot," said Mrs. Younge. "If it must be so," resumed the lady who was inviting us, "let us exchange tokens, and we may meet again." This proposal, so perfectly new to me, was accepted: the fair archers gave our ladies their pearl crescents, which had the appearance of being of considerable value. Madame Younge returned something which I did not see: Mademoiselle Sillery gave a silver Cupid, which had served her for an essence-bottle. The gentleman then shaking hands with us, and the ladies embracing each other, we parted mutually satisfied. "Who are these ladies?" demanded I. "You know them as well as we do," replied Mademoiselle Sillery. "And is it thus," said I, "that you receive all strangers indiscriminately?"—"Yes," replied she; "all strangers of a certain condition. Where they are evidently of our own rank, we know of no reserve. Indeed, why should we? It is to general advantage to be pleased, and to please each other."—"But you embraced them, as if you really felt an affection for them."—"And I did feel that affection for them," said she, "as long as I was with them. I would have done them every service in my power, and would even have made sacrifices to serve them."—"And yet if you were to see them again, you would perhaps not know them."—"Very possibly," replied she. "But I can see no reason why every affection should be necessarily permanent. We never pretend to permanence. We are certainly transient, but not insincere."

In this conversation we reached Ancennis, a village on a green, surrounded by forests. Some of the cottages, as we saw them by moon-light, seemed most delightfully situated, and the village had altogether that air of quietness and of rural retreat, which characterizes the scenery of the Loire. Our horses having preceded us by an hour or more, every thing was prepared for us when we reached our inn. A turkey had been put down to roast, and I entered the kitchen in time to prevent its being spoilt by French cookery. Mademoiselle Sillery had the table provided in an instant with silver forks and table-linen. Had a Parisian seen a table thus set out at Ancennis, without knowing that we had brought all these requisites with us, he would not have credited his senses. The inns in France along the banks of the Loire, are less deficient in substantial comforts than in these ornamental appendages. Poultry is every where cheap, and in great plenty; but a French inn-keeper has no idea of a table-cloth, and still less of a clean one. He will give you food and a feather-bed, but you must provide yourselves with sheets and table-cloths. Our accommodations, with respect to lodging for the night, were not altogether so uncomfortable: the house had indeed two floors, but there were no stairs; so that we had to ascend by a ladder, and that not the best of its kind. There being, moreover, but two rooms, the one occupied by the landlord, his wife, and two grown girls, there was some difficulty as to the disposal of Mademoiselle Sillery and myself. It was at length arranged, that all the females in the house should sleep in one room, and all the males in another. When I came to take possession of my bed, I found that Mrs. Younge had contrived to exempt her husband from this arrangement: he was now sleeping by the side of the handsomest woman in France, whilst I was lying at one end of a dirty room, the other being occupied by the snoring landlord. Fatigue, however, according to the proverb, is better than a bed of down; I accordingly soon fell asleep, and Mademoiselle Sillery was not absent from my dreams. I should not forget to mention, as another specimen of French manners, that I learned from this lady on the following day, that she had slept with her sister and her husband. Such are French manners.

On the following morning, induced by the example of the landlord, and by the beauty of the rising sun, I rose early, and accompanied by my host, walked into the fields round the village. The environs of Ancennis appeared to me extremely beautiful; whether from the mere effect of novelty, or that they really were so, I know not. Some of the neater cottages were situated in gardens very carefully cultivated, and so much in the style of England, that, but for some characteristic frivolities, I could scarcely believe myself in France. In every garden, or orchard, I invariably observed one tree distinguished above the rest; it had usually a seat around its trunk, and where its top was large enough, a railed seat, or what is called in America a look-out, amongst its branches. I had the curiosity to ascend to some of these, for the garden gates were invariably only latched, and small pieces of wood were nailed to the trunk, so as to assist the ascent of the women. The branches, which formed the look-out, were carved with the names of the village beauties, and in one of the seats I found a French novel, and a very pretty paper work-box. I saw enough to conclude, that Ancennis was not without the characteristic French elegance; and I must once for all say, that the manners of Marmontel are founded in nature, and that the daughters of the yeomanry and humbler farmers in France have an elegance, a vivacity, and a pleasantry, which is no where to be found out of France.

On my return I found Mademoiselle Sillery at the breakfast table; and in answer to her inquiries as to the object of my walk, informed her of my observations. She replied, that they were very well founded, and added a reason for it which seemed to me very satisfactory. "The French girls," said she, "all at least who learn to read, are formed to this elegance and softness by the very elements of their education; their class-book is Marmontel, and La Belle Assemblée, the last, one of the prettiest novels in France. They are thus taught love with their letters, and they improve in gallantry as they improve in reading; and I will venture to say," continued this elegant girl, "that by this method of instruction we make a great earned where there is a love-story at the end of it."

We shortly afterwards resumed our progress, and passed through a country of the same kind as on the preceding day, alternate hill and valley. The Arno, as described by the

Tuscan poets, for I have never seen it, must bear a strong resemblance to the Loire from Ancennis to Angers; nothing can be more beautiful than the natural distribution of lawn, wood, hill and valley, whilst the river, which borders this scenery, is ever giving it a new form by its serpentine shape. The favourite images in the landscapes of the ancient painters here meet the eye almost every league: cattle resting under the shade, and attentively eyeing the river, whilst the country around is of a nature and character, which the fancy of a poet would select for the haunt of Dian and her huntresses. The peasantry, as many of them as we met, seemed to have that life and spirits the sure result of comfort; if they were not invariably well clothed, they seemed at least sufficiently so for the climate of the province. The younger women had dark complexions and shining black eyes; their shapes were generally good, and their air and vivacity, even in the lowest ranks, such as peculiarly characterize the French people. If addressed, they were rather obliging than respectful, and had all of them a compliment on their tongues' end. It was not indeed easy to get rid of them with a mere word or question. I must add, however, that I am here describing their manner towards Mr. Younge and myself. Towards the ladies it was somewhat different. When Madame or Mademoiselle spoke to them, they seemed modest and respectful in the extreme; to the latter, indeed, they were more familiar, and many of them, on giving the adieu after a ten minutes' conversation, very prettily embraced her, gently putting their arms round her neck, and kissing the left shoulder; a form of salutation very common in the French provinces. In a word, the more I saw of the French character, the more did I wish that the more weighty and valuable qualities of the English and American character, their honesty and their sincerity, were accompanied by the gentleness, the grace, the affectionate benevolence, which characterise the French manners.

Ingrande, where we dined, is the last town of the province of Bretagne, on the Loire, and thenceforwards we had entered Anjou. It is a town of above three hundred houses, built round the base of a sandy hillock, the church being on the hill. The houses are intermingled with trees, and the country very prettily planted. It is not to be expected that the habitations in such a town could be any thing better than cottages; but they were tolerably clean, and not very ruinous.

We had now passed through the province of Bretagne as it lies along the Loire, and it is but justice to say, that in point of natural scenery, in the wildness and tranquillity which constitute what I should term the romance of landscape, it exceeds every thing in Europe. Along the banks of the Loire, France has meadows, the verdure of which will not sink in comparison with those of England. Along the banks of the Loire, moreover, France has woodlands, and lawns, and an, intermixture of wood and water, and of every possible variety of surface, which no country in the world but France can produce. The Loire is perhaps the only river in Europe which is bordered by hills and hillocks, and which, in so long a course, so seldom passes through a mere dead level. Accordingly, from the earliest times of the French monarchy, the rising grounds of the Loire have been selected for the sites of castles, monasteries, abbeys, and chateaux, and as the possessors have superadded Art to Nature, this natural beauty of the grounds has been improving from age to age. The Monks have been immemorially celebrated for their skill as well in the choice of situations as in their improvement of natural advantages; their leisure, and their taste, improved by learning, have naturally been employed on the scenes of their residence, on their vineyards and their gardens. Innumerable are the still remaining vestiges of their taste and of their industry, and I have a most sincere satisfaction in thus doing them justice; in thus bearing my testimony, that, so far from being the drones of the land, there is no part of a province which they possessed, but what they have improved. The scenery along the Loire has a character which I should think could not be found in any other kingdom, and on any other river. Towns, windmills, steeples, ancient castles and abbeys still entire, and others with nothing remaining but their lofty walls; hills covered with vines, and alternate woods and corn-fields— altogether form a landscape, or rather a chain of landscapes, which remind one of a poem, and successively refresh, delight, animate, and exalt the imagination. Is there any one oppressed with grief for the loss of friends, or what is still more poignantly felt, for their ingratitude and unkindness? Let him traverse the banks of the Loire; let him appeal from man to Nature, from a world of passion and vice, to scenes of groves, meads, and flowers. His must be no common sorrow who would not forget it on the banks of the Loire.

After a short rest at Chantoce, a village of the same rank and character with Mauves, we arrived at Angers, where we proposed to remain till the following Monday, having arrived there on the Thursday evening. We had scarcely reached the inn, before a gentleman of the name of Mons. de Corseult, to whom we had sent forwards our letters from Nantes, addressed himself to us, and insisted that we should continue our journey to his house, about half a mile on the other side of the town. The ladies at length acceded to this proposal, on the condition that our horses, servants, &c. should be sent back to the inn, and that ourselves only should be the visitors of Mons. de Corseult.

## CHAP. XII.

*Angers—Situation—Antiquity and Face of the Town—Grand Cathedral—Markets—Prices of Provisions—Public Walks—Manners and Diversions of the Inhabitants—Departure from Angers—Country between Angers and Saumur—Saumur.*

WE had intended to have reposed ourselves at Angers, but Mons. de Corseult, having been very lately married, had his house daily full of visitors, and as we were strangers, parties were daily made for us. Whatever time I could steal from this unintermitting round, I employed in walks to the town, and in the neighbourhood. Mr. Younge generally accompanied me, but I was sometimes fortunate enough to be honoured with Mademoiselle St. Sillery, an happiness of which I should have been more sensible, had it not usually tempted the intrusion of some coxcomb, who converted a tour of information into a mere lounge of levity and senseless gallantry. How miserable would have been an English girl, of the beauty and wit of this young lady, with such gallants! Or is it with ladies as with the poet in Don Quixotte—are love and flattery sweet, though they may come from a fool and a madman? I should hope not, or at least with Mademoiselle St. Sillery.

In despite, however, of these intrusions, we had two or three pleasant walks through Angers, in which the curiosity of Mademoiselle was of much use to me. He must be less than a man, who could be wearied even by the most minute interrogations of an handsome woman. Mademoiselle St. Sillery, as if resolved to be ignorant of nothing, put the most endless questions to those who accompanied us about the town; and with true French gallantry, the answers even exceeded the questions. I had little to do but to look and to listen.

Angers is situated in a plain, which, in the distance being fringed with wood, and being very fertile in corn and meadow, wants nothing of the richness and beauty which seem to characterize this part of the province. It is parted into two by a river called the Mayenne, which is a small branch of the Loire, and again falls into the main river about five miles from the town. The French, like the Dutch, seemed to be peculiarly attached to this kind of site, having a river run through their towns, one half being built on one side, and one on the other. The water of the Mayenne is so harsh, that it cannot be drunk or used for cookery, and were it not for the proximity of the Loire, and some aqueducts, Angers, though built on a river, must necessarily become desolate for want of water. The same improvidence is visible in many towns in France, and still more in Holland.

The walls round this city were built by King John of England, and though six centuries, have elapsed, are still nearly entire. Part of them were indeed demolished by Louis the Eighth, but they were restored in their original form by his successor, and remain a proof of the durable style of building of that Age (1230). The castle of Angers was built at the same time. It is situated on a rock which overhangs the river, and though now in decay, has still a very striking appearance. The walls are lofty and broad, the towers numerous, and the fosses deep. They are cut out of the solid rock, and must have required long and ingenious labour.

The cathedral of Anjou, the inner part of which exactly resembles Westminster Hall, is chiefly celebrated for containing the monument of Margaret of Anjou, the queen of Henry the Sixth of England. This woman was in every respect a perfect heroine, and worthy of her illustrious father, René, King of Sicily. She was taken prisoner in the battle of Tewkesbury, and immediately committed, to the Tower, from which she was ransomed by Louis the

Eleventh, of France. This King, however, who was never known to forget himself, and act otherwise than selfishly, had a very different motive than humanity for this apparent generosity: having gained possession of the person of Margaret, he immediately rendered her his own prisoner, and caused her father to be informed that if he wished to ransom her, he must give up all his hereditary rights to the duchies of Anjou and Lorrain. So tenderly did René love his daughter, that he made the sacrifice without hesitation. The history of this princess, as collected from the French memoirs, has an air rather of romance than of real history. Though the English historians all concur in her praise, they seem to know very little of her. A remark here suggested itself: that the best of the English historians seem totally to have overlooked all the French records, and to have confined themselves to the writers of their own country.

The general appearance of Angers does not correspond with the magnificence of its walls, its castle, and its cathedral. Its size is respectable; there are six parish churches, besides monasteries and chapters, and the inhabitants are estimated at 50,000. The streets, however, are very narrow, and the houses mean, low, and huddled: there is the less excuse for this, as ground is plentiful and cheap; there is scarcely a good house inhabited within the walls. The towns in France differ in this respect very considerably from those in England: in a principal town in England you will invariably find a considerable number of good houses, where retired merchants and tradesmen live in the ease and elegance of private gentlemen. There is nothing of this kind in the French towns. Every house is a shop, a warehouse, a magazine, or a lodging house. I do not believe that there is one merchant of independent fortune now resident within the walk of Angers. This, indeed, may perhaps arise from the difference in the general character of the two kingdoms: in England, and even in America, there are few tradesmen long resident in a town, without having obtained a sufficiency to retire; whilst the French towns being comparatively poor, and their trade comparatively insignificant, the French tradesman can seldom do more than obtain a scanty subsistence by his business. In all the best French towns, the tradesmen have more the air of chandlers than of great dealers. There are absolutely no interior towns in France like Norwich, Manchester, and Birmingham. In some of their principal manufacturing places, there may indeed be one or two principal men and respectable houses; but neither these men nor their houses are of such number and quality, as to give any dignity or beauty to their towns beyond mere places of trade. The French accordingly, judging from what they see at home, have a very contemptible idea of the term merchant; and if a foreign traveller of this class should wish to be admitted into good company, let him pass by any other name than that of a marchand or negociant. To say all in a word, this class of foreigners are specifically excluded from admission at court.

I visited the market, which in Angers, and I believe throughout France, is held on Sunday. This is one of the circumstances from which a foreigner would be very apt to form a wrong estimate of the French character, which now, whatever it might be, is decidedly religious. But the Roman Catholics have ever considered Sunday as at once a day of festivity and a holiday; they have no scruple, therefore, to sing and dance, and to hold their markets on this day; all they abstain from is the heavier kind of work—labour in the fields and warehouses. A French town, therefore, is never so gay as on a Sunday. I inquired the prices of provisions. Beef and mutton are about 2d. per pound; a fowl 5d.; and turkies, when in season, from 18d. to 2s.; bread is about 1½d. a pound; and vegetables, greens, &c. cheap to a degree. A good house in Angers about six Louis per year, and a mansion fit for a prince (for there are some of them, but without inhabitants) from forty to fifty Louis, including from thirty to forty acres of land without the walls. I have no doubt but that any one might live at Angers on 250 Louis per annum, as well as in England for four times the amount. And were I to live in France, I know no place I should prefer to the environs of this town. The climate, in this part of France, is delightful beyond description. The high vault of heaven is clad in ethereal blue, and the sun sets with a glory which is inconceivable to those who have only lived in more northerly regions; for week after week this weather never varies, the rains come on at once, and then cease till the following season. The tempests which raise the fogs from the ocean have no influence here, and they are strangers likewise to that hot moisture which produces the pestilential fevers in England and America. There are sometimes indeed heavy thunder storms, when the clouds burst, and pour down torrents of rain: but the storm ceases in a few minutes, and the heavens, under the influence of a powerful sun, resume their beauty and serenity.

The soil in the neighbourhood of Angers (I speak still with reference to its aptitude for the residence of a foreigner, for I confess this dream hung very strongly on my imagination) is fertile to a degree, and as far as I could understand, is very cheap. Every house, as I have before said, without the walls, has its garden, and all kind of fruits and vegetables were in the greatest plenty. The fences around the gardens of the villages were very fantastically interwoven with the wreaths of the vine, which would sometimes creep up the trunk of a tree, and sometimes hang over the casements. Nothing can be more delightful than the vine when flourishing in all this unbridled wildness of its natural luxuriance, and as if justly sensible of its beauty, the French cottagers convert it to the double purpose of ornament or utility. Whilst travelling along, my spirits frequently felt the cheering influence of the united images of natural beauty and of human happiness. Often have I seen the weary labourer sitting under a sunny wall, his head shaded by the luxuriant branches of the vine, the purple fruit of which furnished him with his simple meal. Bread and fruit is the constant summer dinner of the peasantry of the Loire. Upon this subject, the general plenty of the country, I should not have forgotten to mention, that in the proper season partridges and hares are in great plenty, and being fed on the heath lands of Bretagne and Anjou, are said to have the best flavour. An Englishman will scarcely believe, that whilst he is paying 12s. a couple for fowls, half a guinea for a turkey, seven shillings for a goose, &c. &c.: whilst such I say are the market prices in London, the dearest price in the market of Angers is 10d. a couple for fowls, a shilling a couple for ducks, 1s. 6d. for a goose. As to the quality of these provisions, the veal and the mutton being fed in the meadows on the Loire, are entirely as good as in England; but the beef, not being in general use except for soups and stews, is of a very inferior kind. Wood is the only article which is dear; but an Englishman in this country would doubtless rise above the prejudices around him, and burn coal, of which there is a great plenty in every part of France.

I must not take leave of Angers without mentioning, that it was a favourite station of the Romans, who, like the monks, always consulted natural beauty in the site of the towns and permanent encampments. Many remnants of this people are still visible: some of the arches of an aqueduct are yet entire, and without a guide speak their own origin.

Accompanied by Mr. Younge and Monsieur de Corseult, I visited the Caserne and the National School. The Caserne was formerly a Riding School of general reputation, and is one of the most superb buildings of the kind in the world. Peter the Great of Russia was here instructed in the equestrian art, and many other illustrious men are on its list of scholars. The National School has nothing worthy of peculiar remark. Angers before the Revolution was celebrated as a seat of literature: its university, founded in 1246, was only inferior to that of Paris; and its Academy of Belles Lettres, founded in 1685, was the first after that of the Nation. The chapel of the university is now a gallery for paintings. The professors of these literary institutions have very competent salaries: the sciences taught are Mathematics, Medicine, Natural and Experimental Philosophy, and the Fine Arts. The best quality, however, of these institutions is that the instructions, such as they are, are gratuitous; the doors are open to all who choose to enter them; those only who can afford it are expected to pay.

Angers, being so near La Vendée, suffered much by the Chouans, and still retains many melancholy traces of the siege which it had to maintain. The people, with feelings which are better conceived than expressed, spoke with great reluctance on their past sufferings: there seems indeed one great maxim at present current in France, and this is to forget the past as if it had never happened. A foreigner is sure to offend, who interrogates them upon any thing connected with the horrible Revolution.

Nothing can be more delightful than the environs of Angers, whether for those who walk or ride. The country is thickly enclosed, and on each side of the river varied with hill and dale, with woodland and meadow. The villages and small towns along the whole bank of the Loire are numerous, and invariably picturesque and beautiful. In the vicinity of Angers the vineyards are very frequent, and cover the hills, and even the valleys, with their luxuriance; nothing can be more beautiful than the natural festoons which are formed by their long branches as they project over the road, and when the grapes are ripe, the landscape wants nothing of perfect beauty. The peasantry, the Vignerons as they are called, live in the midst of their vineyards: their habitations are usually excavated out of the rocks and small hillocks on which they grow their vines, and as these hillocks are usually composed of strata of chalk, the cottages are dry and comfortable. Some of them, as seen from the road, being covered even over their doors by the vine branches, had the appearance of so many nests, and as many of them as had two stories, were picturesque in the extreme. Upon the whole, the condition of the peasantry in this part of France is very comfortable: they are temperate, unceasingly gay, and sufficiently clad; their wants are few, and therefore their labour, added to the fertility of the soil, is sufficient to satisfy them. They repine not for luxuries of which they can have no notion.

We took leave of Monsieur de Corseult on the Wednesday instead of the Monday, but he insisted upon accompanying us on horseback half way to Saumur, where we proposed sleeping. The ladies could not but accept this obliging offer, and the information which Mons. de Corseult was enabled to give us, rendered his society equally agreeable to Mr. Younge and myself. We learned from this gentleman, that though Anjou is reputed to have a great proportion of heath and barren land, it does not yield to any province in France either for beauty or fertility. As much of it as lays along the Loire, I have already had occasion to describe, and what we were now passing through was not a whit behind it. Every village was most romantically situated; some in orchards, some in fenced gardens, some in corn-fields, and others in vales and in recesses on each side of the road. The corn being ripe, added much to the beauty of the landscape. In some fields the reapers were at work, and the harvest was going on with true French gaiety. Sometimes we would see them dancing in the field; sometimes sitting round some central tree sporting and gamboling with the women and girls. I never saw a scene in England which could enter into comparison with a French harvest. I was sorry, however, to see that the women had more than their due share of the labour; they reaped, bound, and loaded. Some of the elder women were accordingly very coarse, but the girls were spirited, and pleasing. They nodded to us whenever we caught their eyes, and if we stopt our horses, would come to us, at whatever distance, as if to satisfy our inquiries.

We happened to pass an estate which was for sale, and the house being at hand, inquired the price and particulars. There were six hundred acres of land, a good house, and the purchase-money was five thousand pounds English. Four hundred acres were arable, the other wood and heath. In England, the price of such an estate would have been at least twenty thousand pounds. The land, though stony, was good, and under the hands of a tolerable farmer, might have cleared the purchase-money in five years. There was a trout stream and fish-ponds, and the whole country was even infested with game. The chateau itself would certainly have required some repairs; it was large and rambling, and seemed to have more wood than brick. The land, however, was richly worth the money four times over.

We reached Saumur very late in the evening; it is a small, but very pretty town, on the southern bank of the Loire. There are here two bridges over the river; the one from the northern shore to an island in the middle of the river; the other from the island to the southern shore. Saumur was formerly a fortified city, and though the fortifications are now neglected and in perfect ruin, it still maintains its rank as a military town, and the names of travellers are formally required, and formally registered. The inn at which we put up was very comfortable; but the beds were so scented with lavender as to prevent me from sleeping. Here likewise, I had the happiness of being again waited upon by females. A young woman, the daughter of the landlord, not only lighted me to my room, but took her seat at the window, and retained it till she saw that I was in bed. The French women have none of that bashful modesty which characterises the women of England and America. Before getting into bed I was about to close a door, which I perceived half open at the extremity of the room opposite to that occupied by my bed; but Felice prevented me, by informing me that her sister and herself were to sleep there, and as a further proof, shewing me the bed. "Then I must leave my own chamber-door open," said I. "Certainly," said she, "if you are not afraid of my sister and me: I have only to see if Madame and Mademoiselle are in want of any thing, and then I shall come to bed." "Where does Mademoiselle sleep?" said I. "In the same chamber with Monsieur and Madame; it is a double-bedded room, on the first floor, fronting the road; you might have observed the casements of it shaded with the barberry tree. But you seem curious as to Mademoiselle. Perhaps there is a *petite affaire* of the heart between you. Well, Heaven bless Monsieur, and may you dream that you are walking with your love in the corn-fields!" Saying this, the sprightly girl left me with the characteristic trip of French gaiety. I had the curiosity to remain awake till her sister and herself passed through my chamber to their own. The girls laughed as they went through the room, and had not even the modesty (for so I must call it) to close their own door. It remained a third part open during the whole night; and as they talked in bed, they prevented my sleep. One of these young women might be twenty; the other, though tall, could not be more than fourteen.

I rose early in the morning with the purpose of a walk in the fields around the town, and finding Felice was going to fetch some milk from a village about half a mile distant, I accompanied her. It is needless to say that she played off all the coquetries which are natural to French girls in whatever station. By dint of frequent questions, however, I collected from her some useful information. I had adopted it as a rule, to obtain information on three points in every French town or village where I might happen to stop—the price of provisions, the price of land, and the price of house-rent. The price of provisions at Saumur, as I learned from this girl, was very cheap: beef, not very good, that is, not very fat, about 1½d. (English) per pound; mutton and veal about 2d.;—two fowls 8d.; two ducks 10d.; geese and turkies from 1s. 6d. to 2s.6d..;—fuel, as much as would serve three fires for the year, about 5l.;—a house of two stories and garrets, two rooms in front and two in back in each story, such being the manner in which they are built, a passage running through the middle, and the rooms being on each side—such a house, resembling an English parsonage, about five Louis a year; or with a garden, paddock, and orchard, about eight Louis;—butter 8d. per pound; cheese 4d.; and milk a halfpenny a quart. According to the best estimate I could make, a family, consisting of a man, his wife, three or four children, two maid-servants, a man-servant, and three horses, might be easily kept at Saumur, and in its neighbourhood, for about 100l. a year. I am fully persuaded that I am rather over than under the mark. The country immediately about Saumur is as lively and beautiful as the town itself. It chiefly consists of corn-fields studded with groves, or rather tufts of trees, and divided by green fences, in which were pear and apple-trees in full bearing. The fields near the town had paths around them and across them, where the towns-folk, as I understood from my informer, were accustomed to walk in the evening and which, the corn being ripe and high, were pleasantly recluse. Felice and myself crossed three or four of them, and if I may judge from the little scrupulosity with which she ran amongst the corn, the proprietors of the lands must gain little from their fields being the customary promenade of their townsmen. One thing, however, I have observed peculiar to the landholders in France—that wherever the free use of their property can contribute in any thing to the enjoyment of others; wherever their fields, or even their parks and gardens, lie convenient for a promenade, those fields, parks, and gardens, are thrown open, and whatever they contain, flowers, fruits, and seats, are all at the public disposal. A Frenchman never thinks of stopping up a bye-path, because it passes within half a mile of his window; a Frenchman never thinks of raising the height of his own wall, in order to interrupt the prospect of his neighbour. One quality, in a few words, pervades all the actions, all the words, and all the thoughts of a Frenchman—a general benevolence, an anxious kindness, which is daily making sacrifices to oblige and even assist others.

Upon my return to the inn, I found Mademoiselle at the breakfast table, which was set in a back room fronting a very pleasant garden. She rallied me pleasantly enough, but as I thought with an air of pique, upon my morning walk and my fair companion, and Felice happening to enter the room, asked her how she should like a foreign husband. "Very well, Mademoiselle," replied the girl with great innocence, "after I had taught him to talk in French: and I believe you are of the same opinion, Mademoiselle," added she with more pertness. Mademoiselle, with true French dexterity, here dropt a cup on the floor, and thus saved the necessity of reply, and furnished an excuse for the confusion into which the girl's impertinence had evidently thrown her. Shall I confess that my vanity was gratified, but I will defy any one to travel through France, without becoming something of a coxcomb.

Having resumed our journey, we proceeded merrily, under a cheering sun refreshed by a morning breeze, on the road for Tours, through les Trois Volets, and Langes. The road was still along the banks of the Loire, and continued on the southern side till we reached Chousay, a very sweet village, about twelve miles from Saumur. We had here a repast of bread, grapes, and a sweet wine peculiar to the country, but the name of which I have not noted; and though together with our servants we drank nearly four quart bottles, and ate a good quantity of grapes and bread, our reckoning did not exceed seven francs. Nothing indeed surprised me so much as the uncommon cheapness in this country. The country to Chousay had a very near resemblance to what we had passed through the preceding day, except that it was more hilly, and the hills being clothed in vines, more beautiful. On some of these hills, moreover, amidst groves or tufts of trees, and lawns extending down the declivity, were some very pretty chateaus, which being white and clean, looked gay and animated. The landscape, indeed, seemed to improve upon us as we advanced; every mile was as charming as the preceding, but every mile began to have a new character. Sometimes the river ran through a plain in which the peasants were gathering in their harvest, to the very brink of the water. Sometimes, the banks on each side were covered with forests, from the centre of which were visible steeples, villas, windmills, and abbeys. At Chousay, I saw the cleanly way in which the Vignerons of the Loire bruise their grapes. In Spain and Portugal, they are put into a mash tub, and the juice is trodden from them by the bare feet of men, women, and girls hired for the purpose: here the practise is to use a wooden pestle. The grapes being collected and picked, are put into a large vat, where they are bruised in the manner I have mentioned, and are thence carried to the press. The vintage had not indeed as yet begun, but I saw the process performed on a small quantity of grapes, which had been ripened in a garden. Every vineyard proprietor, besides his stock-fruit, has some peculiar species of grape from which he makes the wine for his own use and that of his immediate friends: these grapes are very carefully picked and culled, and none but the soundest and best are thrown into the tub. The wine thus made is infinitely superior to the stock-wine for sale: when old, it is not inferior to Hock, and I believe is frequently sold as such by the foreign purchasers.

Our next post was Planchoury, a small village, which we reached about six o'clock in the evening, and where we agreed to remain for the night, that our horses might have a rest, which they seemed to require. Our inn here was a farm-house. We had for our supper a couple of roasted fowls, and a dish which I had never seen before, some new wheat boiled with pepper and salt. It was so savoury, and I have reason to believe so wholesome, that I have frequently taken it since. I can say from experience, that it is a powerful sudorific, and very efficacious in a cold. I must not forget to mention that I slept on some straw, in a kind of hay-oft, and to the best of my memory never slept more delightfully. When I opened my razor case on the following morning, I found a paper, upon unrolling of which I found a ringlet of hair, with the word Felice on the envelope. Once for all, the French women can think of nothing but gallantry, and live for nothing but love. Sweet girl, I will keep thy ringlet, and when weary of the world, will remember thee, and acknowledge that life may still have a charm.

We remained at Planchoury till the noon of the following day, when we resumed our journey, with the intention of dining at Tours. From Planchoury throughout the whole way to Tours, the scenery exceeded all the powers of description. The Loire rolled its lovely stream through groves, meads, and flowers. On both sides was a border of meadow clad in the richest green, varied sometimes by hills which hung over the river, the sides of these hills robed in all the rich livery of the ripening grape, and the towers and battlements of castles just surmounting the woods in which they were embosomed. How delightful must it be to wander in a summer's evening along these lovely banks, far from the din of the distant world, and where the deep tranquillity is only interrupted by the song of the nightingale, the whistle of the swain returning from labour, or the carol of the milkmaid as she is filling her pail. Surely man was formed most peculiarly to relish the charms of Nature. Would Heaven grant me my fondest wish, it would be to wander with * * * * on the banks of the Loire.

45

How sweetly, and even justly, did Felice express the true image of love, when she wished me the golden dream,—that I was wandering with my love in the corn-fields of Saumur.

We passed through Langeais, a small town, celebrated for its melons, with which it supplies Paris, and all France. This town was known to the Romans, by whom it was called Alingavia. We stopped to examine its castle, which is celebrated in the history of France, as the scene of the marriage of Charles the Eighth and Anne of Bretagne. The castle, as may be expected, is now in ruins; but enough remains of it, to prove its former magnificence. It frowns with much sublimity over the subject land. I never remember to have passed through a more lovely country, more varied scenery, abounding in vines, corn, meadow, wood, and water, than the whole of the road between Saumur and Tours. Well might Queen Mary of Scotland exclaim, when leaving the vines and flowers of France for her Scotch kingdom, "Dear, delightful land, must I indeed leave thee! Gay, lovely France, shall I never see thee more!"

We reached Tours somewhat later than we expected. According to our previous arrangement, we were to stay there only the whole of the following day, but we again broke our resolution, and extended our time from one day to three. I envy not that man's heart who can travel France by his watch.

## CHAP. XIII.

*Tours—Situation and general Appearance of it—Origin of the
Name of Huguenots—Cathedral Church of St. Martin—The
Quay—Markets—Public Walk—Classes of Inhabitants—Environs—Expences
of Living—Departure from Tours—Country
between Tours and Amboise.*

WE remained at Tours three days, and though nearly the whole of this time was occupied in an unceasing walk over the town and environs, I was still unwearied, and my subject still unexhausted.

Nothing can be more charming than the situation of this town. Imagine a plain between two rivers, the Loire and the Cher, and this plain subdivided into compartments of every variety of cultivated land, corn-fields studded with fruit-trees, and a range of hills in the distance covered with vineyards to their top, whilst every eminence has its villa, or abbey, or ruined tower. The cities in France, at least those on the Loire, have all somewhat of a rural character; this may be imputed to their comparative want of that trade and manufactures, which in England, and even in America, convert every thing in the vicinity of a town into store-yards. In France, trade has more room than she can well fill, and therefore has no occasion to trespass beyond her limits. There are few towns but have larger quays than their actual commerce requires, and still fewer but what have more manufactories than they have capitals to keep them in work.

The general appearance of Tours, when first entered by a traveller, is brisk, gay, and clean; a great part of it having been burnt down during the reign of the unfortunate Louis, nearly the whole of the main street was laid out and rebuilt at the expence of that Monarch. What before was close and narrow, was then widened and rendered pervious to a direct current of air. The houses are built of a white stone, so as to give this part of the town a perfect resemblance to Bath. Some of them, moreover, are spacious and elegant, and all of them neat, and with every external appearance of comfort. The tradesmen have every appearance of being in more substantial circumstances than is usual with the French provincial dealers; their houses, therefore, are neat and in good repair, the windows are not patched with paper, the wood-work is fresh painted, and the pavement kept clean.

The name of the Huguenots, a party which so fatally divided France during three reigns, originated in one of the gates of this city, which is called the Hugon gate, from Hugo, an ancient count of Tours. In the popular superstition and nursery tales of the country, this Hugo is converted into a being somewhat between a fairy and a fiend, and even the illustrious De Thou has not disdained to make mention of this circumstance: "*Cæsaro duni,*" says this celebrated historian, "*Hugo Rex celebratur, qui noctu Pomœria civitatis obequitare, et obvios homines pulsare et rapere dicitur.*" Be this as it may, the party of the Huguenots, according to

Davila, having originated in this city, they were thence called Huguenots, as a term of derision and reproach.

We visited the cathedral, which, with more decency than in England, is open at all hours of the day, and is not exhibited for money. There might be some excuse for this, where any of the subjects of exhibition are portable, and such as might be carried away. But who would feel any disposition to pilfer the wig of Sir Cloudesley Shovel, or the hat of General Monk, in Westminster Abbey? Why, therefore, is not this disgraceful practice thrown aside? Why is a nation converted into a puppet-show? The English Minister would doubtless be ashamed to bring the returns of these exhibitions amongst the ways and means of the year; yet it is effectually the same to suffer these taxes to be taken as the prices for seeing the public buildings of the nation. There is nothing of this kind in America, or in any other kingdom in the world. The cathedral of Tours has nothing to distinguish it except its antiquity, two beautiful towers, and a library of most valuable manuscripts. Amongst these there is a copy of the Pentateuch, written in the alphabet of the country, upwards of eleven hundred years ago. There is likewise a copy of the four Evangelists, written in Saxon letters, in the beginning of the fifth century, about fifty years after Constantine declared Christianity to be the religion of the Roman Empire. Next to the cathedral, St. Martin's church is usually shewn to strangers. It is the largest church in France, but very dark, damp, and built in a very bad taste. The tomb of St. Martin, whom tradition reports to be buried here, is behind the great Altar; it is of black marble, and though very simple, is very striking. The ancient kings of France used to come to this tomb previous to any of their important expeditions, and after having made the usual prayers of intercession used to take away the mantle of the Saint as the banner under which they were to fight: this mantle still remains.

The quay is broad, brisk, and clean. Even the French merchants seem never to lose sight of the union of pleasure and profit: their quays are terraces, and serve them as well for promenades as for business. One reason, however, for the superiority of the French over the English quays, may be, that the French Government consider these quays as public and national works, and therefore puts them, I believe, under the same system of management as the roads. What Government does, and does with attention, will be done well, because Government consults for the general good; whilst individual proprietors are only actuated by their own immediate interest. If the wharfs and quays on the Thames had been laid out by the English Government, would they have so totally defaced and degraded the banks of that noble river?

There is an excellent market for provisions; I had not the opportunity of seeing it on the market day, but was informed in answer to my inquiries, that every article was plentiful, and very cheap. Wood, which is so dear in every other part of France, is here very cheap, the country being overspread with forests, and the river furnishing a ready transportation. Houses are good and cheap: the rent of a house consisting of a ground floor, two stories above, and attics, the windows in front of each floor being from six to eight, with coach-house, stables, garden and orchards, is about 20*l.* English money, the taxes from 1*l.*10*s.* to 2*l.*, and parish rates about 10*s.* annually. I should not forget to mention, that the gardens are large, sometimes two or three acres, encompassed with high walls, and well planted with fruit-trees, and particularly wall-fruit. In the back part of these gardens are usually gates opening into the fields, which I have before mentioned have walks around and across them, and are the common promenade of all who choose to use them. In the season of harvest or vintage, nothing can be more charming than these walks; the French gaiety and simplicity, not to say puerility, is then seen in all its perfection; it is then a common sport amongst the ladies and the gallants of the town to chase each other amongst the standing corn, and as they endeavour to keep to the furrows, which are too narrow for their feet, the chace is generally terminated by the fall of the runners, the one over the other. The interest of the farmers cannot but suffer by these frolics; but as they participate in the enjoyment, for every one may salute a lady whom he finds in the corn, there is no complaint, and indeed care is taken to do as little mischief as possible. In the summer evenings these fields are almost the sole promenade; and the Mall, or public walk of the town is entirely deserted. On Sundays, however, the Mall has its turn, and all the beauty of the province, and the fashion of the town, may be seen walking up and down this beautiful avenue, being nearly a mile and half in length, and planted on both sides with ranges of elms apparently almost as ancient as the town. The magistrates are so careful of this ornament of their town, that they suffer no one to walk there after rain, and penalties are imposed on every species of nuisance or abuse.

The society of Tours is infinitely beyond that of any other provincial town in France. I have already mentioned, that there are some excellent houses within the city, and they are in great numbers in the immediate vicinity. Tours, in this respect, resembles Canterbury or Salisbury, in England. It is the favourite retreat of such advocates as have made fortunes in their profession. The noblesse of the province have their balls and assemblies almost weekly during the summer months; and even in the winter, Tours is by many preferred to Paris. It would be an unpardonable omission, whilst I am upon this subject, not to notice the uncommon beauty of the younger women; a beauty, the effect of which is much raised by their vivacity, and unwearied gaiety. Love and gallantry seem the main business of the town, and whilst we were there, we were amused with two or three stories of infidelities on all sides. There is a very pretty custom at their balls: if a lady accepts a partner, she presents him, if in summer, with a flower; if in winter, with a ribbon of what she has adopted as her colour. Every unmarried lady has a colour which she has adopted as her own, and which she always wears on some part of her dress.

Tours was formerly celebrated for its silk manufactory, and enough of it still remains to invite and to gratify the curiosity of a traveller. The attention of the French Government is now unintermittingly occupied in efforts to raise the manufactures of the kingdom, but whilst the war makes such large demands, trade must necessarily be cramped. The manufactories, however, still continue to work, and produce some beautiful flowered damasks, and brilliant stuffs. The weavers for the most part work at their own houses, and have so much by the piece, the silk being furnished them by their employers. The prices vary with the pattern and quality of the work; two livres per day is the average of what can be earned by the weavers. The women weave as well as the men, and their earnings may be estimated at about one half. Upon the whole, however, these manufactures are in a very drooping condition, and are scarcely visible to a foreign visitant, unless the immediate object of his inquiry. There is likewise a ribbon manufactory, but the ribbons are very inferior to those of England. About 1000 persons may be employed in these two manufactories.

We visited the castle of Plessis les Tours, which is not more than a mile from the city. This chateau was built by that execrable tyrant, Louis the Eleventh, was his constant residence during his life-time, and the scene of his horrible death. This monarch is one of those whom all concur in mentioning with execration; Richard of England has found apologists in this ingenious age, but no one has come forward to defend the memory of the French Tiberius. The castle is built of brick, and is very pleasantly situated, being surrounded by woods. In the chapel is a portrait of Louis the Eleventh; he is painted as in the act of saluting the Virgin Mary, and our Saviour as an infant. His features are harsh, and something of the tyrant is legible even through the adulation of the painter. The castle, though built about 1450, is still perfect in all its parts, and has some large apartments.

I believe I have already mentioned, that when I had occasion to stop in any town, which I thought had a *primâ facie* appearance of being a place of pleasant residence or settlement for a foreigner, the main object of my inquiries went to ascertain all those points which were necessary to determine this question. Of all the cities which I had yet seen, Tours appeared to me the best adapted for such a residence. The country is delightful and healthy, the society good, and every necessary article of life plentiful and cheap. Beef, veal, and mutton, are to be had in great plenty, and the two latter excellent. Poultry is equally plentiful and cheap. Fuel, to those who have horses, amounts almost to nothing; house-rent likewise very reasonable. Land in purchase about 15*l.* per acre, one with another—wood, heath, and arable. In the immediate neighbourhood of the town the meadow land is dear. I believe I have now mentioned every thing. Young persons would find Tours a delightful residence, as there is a never-ceasing course of balls and parties. A carriage may be kept cheaply; in a word, I would venture positively to say, that for 250*l.* English money annually, a family might live at Tours in plenty and elegance; but let them not have English or American servants.

Having seen enough of Tours, we resumed our journey after our breakfast on the third day, proposing to go no farther on that day than Amboise, a distance short of twenty miles. Every traveller must have observed, that the exhilaration of the animal spirits is never greater than after an interval of fatigue succeeded by sufficient repose. A spirited horse, for example, will perform his second stage, after a sufficient bait, with more animation than his first: it is the same with travellers, or at least I must assert it of myself. My satisfaction is always greater in the progress, than in the commencement of a journey. There is a dilatoriness, a *vis inertiæ*, which hangs on me on my first departure, and which does not pass away, till worked off by the fermentation of the blood and spirits.

The whole party, and myself amongst the number, left Tours in this enviable state of spirits; the sun shone brightly, but a refreshing breeze, and intervals of the road well shaded, softened an heat, which might otherwise have been oppressive. Mr. Younge and myself rode on each side of the carriage, and travelling slowly, as our proposed day's journey was short, enjoyed at once the scenes of nature, and the conversation of these lovely women.

"The next village we shall come to," said Mademoiselle St. Sillery, "will be a singularity. Unless we were with you, you might perhaps pass through it without seeing it. You might pass through the midst of three or four hundred inhabitants without seeing either house, man, woman, or child."

"You are speaking of Mont Louis," said Mr. Younge.

"Yes," replied Mademoiselle, "but I will not anticipate Monsieur's gratification by more fully informing him."

Mr. Younge, in the course of this conversation, gave me some important information with respect to the climate of this part of France. I have entered it in my note book as nearly as possible in his own words, and therefore shall give it as such.

"If an American, an English, or a Swedish gentleman, wished to settle in France," said he, "I would recommend above all provinces either Tourraine or the Limosin. What the country is as to natural beauty, and as to fertility of soil, you may see through every league; it is that mixture of the wild and of the cultivated, of the field, of the wood, of the vineyard, and of the garden, which is not to be equalled in Europe, and which has rendered this part of France the favourite of painters and poets from time immemorial. Here the Troubadours have built their fairy castles, have settled their magicians, and bound their ladies in enchanted gardens; and even the popular superstition of the country seems to have taken its tone and colour from the images around. Tourraine, and all the country on the banks of the Loire, has a kind of popular mythology of its own; it is the land of fairies and elfins, and there is scarcely a glen, a grove, or a shady recess, but what has its tale belonging to it. What one of the French poets has said of the Seine, may be said with more truth of the Loire—all its women are queens, and all its young men poets. If Mademoiselle St. Sillery were speaking," continued he, smiling at this young lady, "she would say, that love reigned triumphant amidst the charms of Nature.

"The climate exactly corresponds to this singular beauty of the country. In many years there is no such thing as snow, and frosts are not frequent, and never severe. The rainy weather comes usually at once, and is confined to the spring. There are no fogs and vapours as is usual in the northern kingdom: the spring is a continuance of such weather as is seen in England about the middle of May. The harvest begins about the latter end of June, but is sometimes so late as the middle of July; it continues a month. The vent de bize is very rare in these provinces. The great heats are from the middle of July to the middle of August During this time, the climate of Touraine certainly exceeds any thing that is common in England. The heaths are covered with thyme, lavender, rosemary, and the juniper-tree: nothing can be more delightful than the scent of them, when the wind blows over them. The hedges are every where interspersed with flowers; there are blossoms of some kind or other throughout the year. I must not, however, disguise from you, that there are some drawbacks from this excellence: the countries south of the Loire are subject to violent storms of rain and hail, and the latter particularly is occasionally so violent, as to beat down and destroy all the corn and vintage on which it may fall. These hail-storms, however, at least in this excessive degree, are not very frequent; they sometimes do not occur once in five years. Some years ago, they were more frequent than they are at present: they used to come on at that time with a

49

violence which swept every thing before them, even destroying the cattle, and it is said that even men have been killed by these hail-stones. Such storms, however, are now considered as natural phenomena.

"The plenty of these provinces, I speak of Touraine and Anjou, is such as might be expected from their climate, and the fertility of the soil. I am persuaded, that a family or an individual might live at one-fourth of the expence which it would cost them either in England or in America. Bread is cheaper by two-thirds, and meat of all kinds is about one-fourth of the London market. Land, both in rent and purchase, is likewise infinitely cheaper than in England, and if managed with any skill, would replace its purchase-money in seven years. The French farmers, for want of capital, leave half their land totally uncultivated, and the other half is most scandalously neglected. An English farmer would instantaneously double or quadruple the produce of the province. The government, moreover, admits foreigners of any country as denizens, under the condition that they shall apply themselves to agriculture or manufactures. I am not, however, certain that agriculture is included in this permission, but I am inclined to believe that it is comprehended in it. Of one thing I am sure, that the government would not refuse its protection, and if required, its special licence, to any foreign agriculturist, who should be desirous of purchasing and settling."

In this and similar conversation we reached Mont Louis, and it exactly answered the description which the ladies had given of it. We were in the midst of the village and its inhabitants before we saw it. Imagine a number of sandy hills on each side of the road, and the sides of them scooped out into houses or rather caves, and you have a sufficient idea of this French village, containing some hundreds of inhabitants. The hills being hollowed out on the further extremity from the road, a traveller might certainly pass through it, without perceiving any thing of it. This style is even carried where there is not the same natural advantage of a hill to hollow out. The village extends into the plain, which is likewise dug out into subterraneous houses, and which are only visible by the smoke issuing from the chimnies. I could not understand the convenience or necessity for these kind of habitations. The ground, indeed, being chalky, is at once dry and easily dug, but on the other hand, the country so abounds in wood and clay, that a very little industry, and a very little expence, might have provided these living human beings with something better than a grave. Mademoiselle St. Sillery, however, made a remark which I must not pass over. "You must not," said this lady, "necessarily infer the misery of our peasantry, because you see them in such unfit habitations. When you compare the French poor, with the poor in your own country, you must take all circumstances with you. When you see the French peasantry so ill lodged, and so scantily clad, you must bring into your view at the same time the difference of the climate. Here, the same sun which now shines upon us, shines on us the whole year round; our rains are short, and all confined to their season; we know nothing of the northern damps: a piece of muslin or fine linen hung in one of those caves for six months, would be dry and unsullied when removed. Those caves, moreover, bad as they are, belong to their inhabitants; the property is their own. Can your peasantry say the same? Believe me, Monsieur, there are many very happy, aye and very lovely faces, under those turf dwellings."

We reached Amboise in good time, and as we intended leaving it on the following morning, Mr. Younge and myself walked over the town, in the interval between dinner and tea. The ladies reserved themselves for the promenade, which in the provincial towns usually begins at seven, and continues till nine.

Amboise, like all the towns on the Loire, is very pleasantly situated, but has nothing in its structure to recommend it to particular notice. It consists of two streets and a chateau. Before the Revolution it was very singularly divided into two parishes and two churches: all gentlemen, all military officers, all landed proprietors who possessed honorary fiefs, and all strangers who were temporary residents, were considered as belonging to one parish, and the people and the bourgeois were attached to the other. The Revolution has annihilated these absurd distinctions, and every one now belongs to the parish in which he resides, or has property.

We visited the chateau, or castle, which is indeed well worthy of the particular attention of travellers. It is built upon a lofty and craggy rock, and overhangs the Loire, which flows at the bottom; the side on the Loire is perpendicular, and of great height, so as to render it almost inaccessible. This vast structure was not all the work of one time, or of one author. The present castle was built upon the ruins of one which was destroyed by the Normans in the year 882, but having gone into decay, was repaired and enlarged by Francis the First and Charles the Eighth. The latter prince was born in this castle, and during his whole reign it was the constant summer residence of the court. The most remarkable part of this structure is what is called the oratory of Louis the Wicked; it is at a great depth beneath the foundation of the castle, and the descent to it is by spiral or well-stairs. It is literally nothing more than a dungeon, on a platform, in which is a prostrate statue representing the dead body of our Lord, as taken from the Cross, covered with streaks of blood, and the skin in welts, as if fresh from the scourge. According to the tradition of the neighbourhood, this was the daily scene of the private devotions of Louis the Eleventh; and the character of the place and of the images around, have certainly some symphony with the known disposition of that monarch. No one, even in the horrible Revolution, has disturbed these relics; it is still exhibited as the tyrant's dungeon, and no one enters or leaves it without feeling a renewed idea of the character of that execrable monster.

The conspiracy of Amboise having originated in this city, the walls and dungeons of the castle still retain some relics of the ferocious cruelties exercised by the triumphant party of the Guises. Spikes, nails, and short iron gibbets and chains, are still shewn on the walls, on which were suspended the bodies of the prisoners who fell into their hands. How difficult is it to reconcile such ferocity to the known greatness of the Duke of Guise; but religious fury has no limits, and a true enthusiast comforts himself that he tortures the body to save the soul. Thank Heaven, that the days of such infuriate zeal are over: but Heaven forbid that we should pass to the other extreme. Great as may be the evils of bigotry, the mischief of religious indifference, or in other words, of no religion at all, would be infinitely greater. The one may affect the world as a storm, the other is a perpetual pestilence, beneath the influence of which every thing that is generous and noble, morals, and even private honor, must fall to the ground.

### CHAP. XIV.

*Lovely Country between Amboise and Blois—Ecures—Beautiful*
*Village—French Harvesters—Chousi—Village Inn—Blois—*
*Situation—Church—Market—Price of Provisions.*

ON the following morning we resumed our journey for Blois, a distance of thirty miles, which we proposed to reach the same day.

The country for some leagues very nearly resembled that through which we had passed on the preceding day, except that it was more thickly spread with houses, and better cultivated. Windmills are very frequent along the whole line of the Loire, the wheat of the country being ground in the vicinity of the river, so as to be more convenient for transportation. These mills are beautifully situated on the hills and rising grounds, and add much to the cheerfulness of the scenery. The road, moreover, was as various as it was beautiful. Sometimes it passed through open fields, in which the peasantry were at work to get in their harvest. Upon sight of our horses, the labourers, male and female, ceased from their work, and ran up to the carriage: some of the younger women would then present us with some wheat, barley, or whatever was the subject of their labour, accompanying it with rustic salutations, and more frequently declining than accepting any pecuniary return. This conduct of the French peasantry is a perfect contrast to what a traveller must frequently meet in America, and still more frequently in England. Amongst the inferior classes in England and America, to be a stranger is to be a subject for insult. So much I must say in justice for the French of the very lowest condition, that I never received any thing like an insult, and that they no sooner understood me to be a stranger, than they were officious in their attentions and information.

I enquired of Mr. Younge what were the wages of the labourers in this part of France. "Their wages," said he, "are very different according to the season. In harvest-time, they have as much as 36 sols, about 1s. 6d.English money. The average daily wages of the year may amount to 24 sols, or a shilling English; they are allowed moreover, three pints of the wine of the country. Their condition is upon the whole very comfortable: the greater part of

51

them have a cow, and a small slip of land. There is a great deal of common land along the whole course of the Loire, and the farmers have a practice of exchanging with the poor. The poor, for example, in many districts, have a right of commonage, during a certain number of days, over all the common fields; the farmers having possession of these lands, and finding it inconvenient to be subject to this participation, frequently buy it off, and in exchange assign an acre or more to every collage in the parish. These cottages are let to the labourers for life at a mere nominal rent, and are continued to their families, as long as they remain honest and industrious. There is indeed no such thing as parochial taxes for the relief of the poor, as in England, but distress seldom happens without being immediately relieved."

"In what manner," said I, "do the French poor live?"

"Very cheaply, and yet all things considered, very sufficiently. You, who have lived almost the whole of your life in northern climates, can scarcely form any idea, what a very different kind of sustenance is required in a southern one. In Ireland, however, how many robust bodies are solely nourished on milk and potatoes: now chesnuts and grapes, and turnips and onions in France, are what potatoes are in Ireland. The breakfast of our labourers usually consists of bread and fruit, his dinner of bread and an onion, his supper of bread, milk, and chesnuts. Sometimes a pound of meat may be boiled with the onion, and a bouillé is thus made, which with management will go through the week. The climate is such as to require no expence in fuel, and very little in clothes."

In this conversation we reached Ecures, a village situated on a plain, which in its verdure, and in the fanciful disposition of some trees and groves, reminded me very strongly of an English park. This similitude was increased by a house on the further extremity of the village: it was situated in a lawn, and entirely girt around by walnut trees except where it fronted the road, upon which it opened by a neat palisadoed gate. I have no doubt, though I had no means of verifying my opinion, that the possessor of this estate had been in England. The lawn was freshly mown, and the flowers, the fresh-painted seats, the windows extending from the ceiling to the ground, and even the circumstance of the poultry being kept on the common, and prevented by a net-work from getting on the lawn—all these were so perfectly in the English taste, that I offered Mr. Younge any wager that the possessor had travelled. "He is most probably a returned emigrant," said Mr. Younge; "it is inconceivable how much this description of men have done for France. The government, indeed, begins to understand their value, and the list of the proscribed is daily diminishing."

From Ecures to Chousi the country varies very considerably. The road is very good, but occasionally sandy. To make up for this heaviness, it is picturesque to a degree. The fields on each side are so small as to give them a peculiar air of snugness, and to suggest the idea to a traveller, how delightful would be a fancy-cottage in such a situation. For my own part, I was continually building in my imagination. These fields were well enclosed with thick high hedges, and ornamented with hedge-rows of chesnut and walnut trees. There were scarcely any of them but what had a foot-path on the side of the road; in others there were bye-paths which led from the road into the country, sometimes to a village, the chimnies only of which were visible; at other times to a chateau, the gilded pinnacle of which shone afar from some distant hill. I observed several fields of flax and hemp, and we passed several cottages, in the gardens of which the flax flourished in great perfection, Mr. Younge informed me, that every peasant grew a sufficient quantity for his own use, and the females of his family worked them up into a strong, but decent looking linen. "This is another circumstance," said he, "which you must not forget in your comparison between the poor of France and other kingdoms. The French peasantry, and particularly the women, have more ingenuity than the English or American poor; they universally make every thing that is connected with their own clothes. Their beds, blankets, coats, and linen of all kind, are of the manufacture of their own families. The produce of the man's labour goes clear to the purchase of food: the labour of his wife and daughters, and even a small portion of their labour, is sufficient to clothe him and to provide him with his bed."

We passed several groups of villagers reposing themselves under the shade: I should not indeed say reposing, for they were romping, running, and conversing with all the characteristic merriment of the country. They saluted us respectfully as we passed them. In one of these groups was a flageolet-player; he was piping merrily, his comrades accompanying the tune with motions of their hands and neck. "Confess," said Mademoiselle St. Sillery, "that we are a happy people: these poor creatures have been at their labour since sunrise, and yet this is the way they repose themselves." "Are they never wearied?" said I. "Never so much so, but what they can sing and dance: their good-humour seems to hold them in the stead of the more robust nerves of the north. Even labour itself is not felt where the mind takes its share of the weight."

"You are a philosopher," said Mr. Younge to her, smiling.

"I am a Frenchwoman," replied she, "and would not change my cheerful flow of spirits for all the philosophy and wisdom in the universe. Nothing can make me unhappy whilst the sun shines."

I know not whether I have before mentioned, that a great quantity of maize is cultivated in this part of the kingdom. The roofs of the cottages were covered with it drying in the sun; the ears are of a bright golden yellow, and in the cottage gardens it had a beautiful effect. I observed moreover a very striking difference between the system of cultivating the flax in England and in France. In England the richest land only is chosen, in France every soil indiscriminately. The result of this difference is, that the flax in France is infinitely finer than in England, a circumstance which may account for the superiority of their lawns and cambrics.

We reached Chousi to an early dinner. The woman of the house apologised that she had no suitable room for so large a company, "but her husband and sons were gathering apples in the orchard, and if we would dine there, we should find it cheerful enough." We readily adopted this proposal, and had a very pleasant dinner under an apple tree. Mademoiselle and myself had agreed to divide between us the office of purveyor to the party. It was my part to see that the meat or poultry was not over-boiled, over-hashed, or over-roasted, and it was her's to arrange the table with the linen and plate which we brought with us. It is inconceivable how much comfort, and even elegance, resulted from this arrangement.

Mr. Younge and myself being engaged in an argument of some warmth, in which Mrs. Younge had taken part, Mademoiselle St. Sillery had given us the slip, and the carriage being ready, I had to seek her. After much trouble I found her engaged in a childish sport with some boys and girls, the children of the landlord: the game answered to what is known in America by the name of hide and seek, and Mademoiselle St. Sillery, when I found her, was concealed in a *saw-pit*. I have mentioned, I believe, that this young lady was about twenty years of age; an elegant, fashionable girl, and as far removed from a romp and a hoyden as it is possible to conceive; yet was this young lady of fashion now engaged in the most puerile play, and even seemed disappointed when she was called from it. Such is the French levity, that sooner than not be in motion, the gravest and most dignified of them would join in an hunt after a butterfly. I have frequently been walking, with all possible gravity, with Mademoiselle St. Sillery, when she has suddenly challenged me to run a race, and before I could recover my astonishment, or give her an answer, has taken to her heels.

We reached Blois rather late; we had intended to have staid there only the night, but as it was too late to see the town, and the following morning was showery, we remained there the whole day, and very pleasantly passed the afternoon in walking over the town, and informing ourselves of its curiosities. The situation of Blois is as agreeable as that of all the other principal towns on the Loire. The main part of it is built upon an hill which descends by a gentle declivity to the Loire; the remaining part of it is a suburb on the opposite side of the river, to which it is joined by a bridge resembling that at Kew, in England. From the hill on which the town stands is a beautiful view of a rich and lovely country, and there is certainly not a town in France or in Europe, with the exception of Tours and Toulouse, which can command such a delightful landscape. It appeared, perhaps, more agreeable to us as we saw it after it had been freshened by the morning rain. The structure of the town does not correspond with the beauty of its site. The streets are narrow, and the houses low. There are some of the houses, however, which are very respectable, and evidently the habitation of a superior class of inhabitants. They reminded me much of what are common in the county towns of England.

But the boast and ornament of Blois is its chateau, or castle. We employed some hours in going over it, and I shall therefore describe it with some fullness.

The situation of it is extremely commanding, and therefore very beautiful. It is built upon a rock which overhangs the Loire, all the castles upon this river being built with the evident purpose of controuling and commanding the navigation. What first struck us very forcibly was the variety and evident dissimilarity of the several parts. This circumstance was explained to us by our guide, who informed us that the castle was the work of several princes. The eastern and southern fronts were built by Louis the Twelfth about the year 1520, the northern front was the work of Francis the First, and the western side of Gaston, duke of Orleans. Every part accordingly has a different character. What is built by Louis the Twelfth is heavy, dark, and gothic, with small rooms, and pointed arches. The work of Francis the First is a curious specimen of the Gothic architecture in its progress, perhaps in its very act of transit, into the Greek and Roman orders; and what has been done by Gaston, bears the character of the magnificent mind and bold genius of that great prince. This comparison of three different styles, on the same spot, gave me much satisfaction.

The rooms, as I have said, such as were built by Louis the Twelfth, are small, and those by Francis spacious, lofty, and boldly vaulted. Nothing astonished me more than the minor ornaments on the points of the arches; they were so grossly, so vulgarly indecent, that I was fearful the ladies might observe me as I looked at them: but such was the taste of the age. Others of the ornaments were less objectionable: they consisted of the devices of the several princes who had resided there.

We were shewn the chamber in which the celebrated Duke of Guise was assassinated, and the guide pointed out the spot on which he fell. A small chamber, or rather anti-chamber, leads to a larger apartment: the Duke had passed through the door of this anti-chamber, and was opening the further door which leads into the larger apartment, when he was assassinated by order of Henry the Third. His body was immediately dragged into the larger apartment, and the king came to view it. "How great a man was that!" said he, pointing to his prostrate body. Historians are still divided on the quality of this act, whether it is to be considered as a just execution, or as a cowardly assassination. Considering the necessary falsehood, and breach of faith, under which it must have been perpetrated, the moralist can have no hesitation to execrate it as a murder.

We passed from this part of the castle to the tower at the western extremity, called La Tour de chateau Regnaud, and so called, because a seigniory of that name, though distant twenty-one miles, is visible from its summit. The Cardinal of Guise, being seized on the same day in which his brother was assassinated, was imprisoned in this castle, and after passing a night in the dungeons, was executed on the day following. The dungeons are the most horrible holes which it is possible to conceive: the descent to them entirely indisposed us from going down. Imagine a dark gloomy room, itself a horrible dungeon, and in the centre of the floor a round hole of the size and shape of those on the paved footpaths in the streets in London for shooting coals into the cellars. Such is the descent to these dungeons: and in such a place did the great and proud Cardinal of Guise terminate a life of turmoil and ambition.

We next visited the Salle des Etats, or the States-hall, so called because the States General were there assembled by Henry the Third: it is a large and lofty room, but the part of it which chiefly attracts the attention of travellers is the fire-place, where the bodies of the Guises were reduced to ashes on the day following their murder. It is not however easy to conceive, why vengeance should be carried so far.

The western front of the castle, which was built by Gaston, Duke of Orleans, is in every respect worthy of that great prince, and of the architect employed by him, the illustrious Mansard. This architect laboured three years upon this front, and having already spent three hundred and thirty thousand livres, informed the prince, that it would require one hundred thousand more to render it habitable. The prince, however eager both to encourage the artist and to have the work finished, could not muster up the money, which in that age was an immense sum: the front, therefore, was left in the state in which it now remains. It is as much to the credit of the Duke as to that of the architect, that this noble front constituted his pride, and that he felt the value of this work of Mansard.

54

The gardens of the castle are worthy of the structure to which they are attached: Henry the Fourth divided them by a gallery into the upper and lower gardens, but nothing now remains of this gallery but the ruins. The garden itself is now sold or let to private persons.

Blois has several other buildings which are worthy of the attention of a leisurely traveller: amongst these is the college, which formerly belonged to the Jesuits, and which is at present a national school. The church attached to the college combines every order of architecture: there are two splendid monuments, moreover, the one to Gaston Duke of Orleans, the other to a daughter of this prince. The courts, likewise, in which the police is administered, are not unworthy of a cursory attention; they are very ancient, having been built by the former Counts of Blois.

We were shewn likewise the aqueducts: the waters rise from a deep subterraneous spring, and are conveyed in a channel cut in a rock. This channel is said to be of Roman construction, and from its characteristic boldness, and even greatness, it most probably is so. Whence is it, that this people communicated their characteristic energy even to trifles. The channel of the aqueduct empties itself into a reservoir adjoining the city walls, whence they are distributed in pipes through all quarters of the city.

## CHAP. XV.
*Houses in Chalk Hills—Magnificent Castle at Chambord—Return from Chambord by Moon-light—St. Laurence on the Waters.*

ON the following morning we resumed our journey. The country continued very similar to that through which we had previously past, except that it was more populous, and there were a greater number of chateaus. On some parts of the road, the chalk hills on the side of the river presented a very curious spectacle: smoke issued out of an hundred vents on the sides and summits, and gave them the appearance of so many volcanoes. The fact was, that the descent fronting the river was scooped into houses or rather caves for the peasantry, and the roof was cut upwards for the chimney. I was informed by Mr. Younge, that the other circumstances of these houses and their inhabitants did not correspond with the implied poverty in their construction. "The fronts of these cottages," said he, "are very picturesque; they have casements, and the walls are deeply shaded and embossed with vines. These caverns are in some places in rows one above another. They are not all of them the property of those who live in them: some of them are constructed at the expence of the farmers, and are let out at a yearly hire of four or five livres. The fronts are masonry: the small gardens which you see above, belong to these cottagers; many of them have moreover a cow, which they feed in the lanes and woods. Altogether, their condition is more comfortable than you would imagine."

As the distance between Blois and Orleans was too much for one day, we had divided it into two, and arranged it so as to comprehend Chambord in the first. This route indeed was considerably out of our direct way, but Mr. and Mrs. Younge resolved that I should see Chambord, and would hear of no excuses.

In pursuance of this plan we turned out of the main road, and entered a narrow one, which by its recluseness and solitude seemed to lead us into the recesses of the country. Nothing can be more beautiful than these bye-roads both in France and England. On the highways, and in the vicinity or route of central and populous towns, the spirit of improvement, and the caprice of wealth, too frequently destroy the scenes of nature: the artist in fashion is set at work, and the field and the meadow is supplanted by the park, the lawn, and the measured avenue. In the bye-lanes, on the contrary, the country is generally left in its natural rudeness, and therefore in its natural beauty: no one thinks of improving the house, orchard, and fields of his tenant; no one cares whether his gates are painted, or his hedges are trim and even. The bye-road, therefore, has always been my favourite haunt; and if ever I should make a pedestrian tour through Europe, I should go in a track very different from any who have gone before.

The scenery in this cross-road to Chambord, as to its general character, was exactly what I had anticipated; recluse and romantic to the most extreme degree. The fields were small, and thickly enclosed; nothing could be more beautiful than the shocks of corn as seen through the thick foliage of the hedges. "How pleasant," said Mademoiselle to me, "would be a walk by sunset under those hedge-rows." I agreed in the observation, and repeat it as conveying an idea of the character of the scenery. The gates and stiles to these several fields seemed as if they had been made by Robinson Crusoe: there is nothing in America more rough and aukward. We passed several cottages very delightfully situated, and without a single exception covered with grapes. The gradual approach to them had something which spoke both to the imagination and the feelings. Imagine the carriage driving very slowly onwards, when you suddenly hear a sweet female voice carrolling away in all the wildness of nature, and this without knowing whence it comes. On a sudden, coming nearer the bottom of the hill, you see on one side of the road a cottage chimney, peeping as it were from a tuft of trees in a dell, and immediately afterwards, coming in front, behold a girl picking grapes for the press, and chearfully singing over her toil. There are few of these cottages but what have a garden fronting the road, and some of these gardens, in the season of fruit and flowers, are inimitably beautiful. Where is it that I have read, that a Frenchman has no idea of gardening? Nothing can be more false: the French peasants infinitely excell the English of the same order in the knowledge and practice of this embellishment.

Nothing can be more obscure, more melancholy, than the situation of Chambord; it is literally buried in woods, and the building, immense as it is, is not visible till you are within some hundred yards of it. The woods are not merely on one side, but entirely surround it, leaving only a park in front, through the midst of which slowly flows a narrow river. The day was overclouded, and I think I never beheld a more melancholy scene.

The style of building is strictly Gothic, and the architecture, considering the order, is very good. It was built by Francis the First, who, on his return from Spain, commanded the ancient chateau of the Counts of Blois to be destroyed, and built this in its place. He is said to have employed eighteen hundred workmen for twelve years, and even then it was left unfinished. It is moated and walled round, and has every appendage of the Gothic castle, innumerable towers and turrets, drawbridges and portals. If seated upon an hill, it would be impossible to conceive a finer object.

The apartments correspond with its external magnitude; they are large and spacious, but the effect of them is destroyed by what is very common in old Gothic buildings; cross-beams from one side of the room to the other. There is a silly story, that Catherine of Medicis had them so placed by the advice of an astrologer, who having cast her nativity discovered that she was in danger of perishing by the fall of an house. The great Marshal Saxe lived and died in this chateau: the room in which he breathed his last, is still shewn with great veneration. There is a tradition that he was killed in a duel by the Prince of Conti, and that his death was concealed. The Marshal lived here in great state; he had a regiment of 1500 horse, the barracks of which are in the immediate vicinity of the castle. The apartments which he occupied are in very good taste; the ceilings are arched, and the proportions are excellent. In one of the rooms is an admirable picture of Louis the Fourteenth on horseback. The spiral staircase is a contrivance which it is impossible to explain; it is so managed, as to contain two distinct staircases in one, so that people may go up and down at the same time, without seeing each other. The apartments are said to exceed twelve hundred.

This castle was the favourite residence of Francis the First, and it was here that he so magnificently received and entertained the Emperor Charles the Fifth. Francis the First was in every respect a true French Knight; gallant, magnificent, and religious in the extreme. There was formerly a pane of glass in one of the windows of this chateau, on which Francis the First had written the two following lines;

Toute                                      Femme                                      varie,
Mal Habil qui s'y fie.

This glass is now lost, and I transcribe the verses from a detailed description of this chateau published at Paris. The castle has been deserted since the death of Louis the Fourteenth. This monarch used occasionally to hunt in its forests, but never made it a permanent residence.

We proposed to sleep at St. Laurence on the Waters, a beautiful village on the high road to Orleans, and distant about twelve miles from Chambord. It was evening before we left the castle, and the moon, though not at the full, had risen, before we had performed the half our road. Nothing could be more picturesque than the scenery, as now half illuminated and half shaded. The cottage gardens looked like so many fairy scenes. The peasant girls looking out of their windows, as they were going to bed, added much to our mirth; and more particularly, as our carriage was on a level with their windows. Whether the moon suited their complexions better than the sun, or that they were different individuals from those we had passed in the morning, I know not, but so much I can say, that they appeared to me more delicate and beautiful. One girl had the face of an angel: it is still imprinted on my mind, and were I a painter, I could exhibit a most perfect resemblance of her, by transferring the copy from my imagination to the canvass. There are some faces which it is impossible to forget.

We passed a group of gipsies: they were seated under a broad branching oak by the road-side; there were twenty or more of them collected in a circle, in the midst of which was a fire, and a pot boiling. "These people," said Mademoiselle St. Sillery, "are realising the wish of our good King Henry the Fourth: he wished that every peasant in France might have a fire in his chimney, and a fowl in his pot:—— and fowls must be very scarce, when these good folks are in want of them."

"Whence is it," said I, "that such notorious thieves are tolerated."

"From the humanity," said Mr. Younge, "which prevails from an indistinct reference to their origin. They are generally considered as the refugees from some persecution in their native land: they have fled from towns and cities to the shelter of woods and fields. On the continent they are almost universally called Bohemians, and regarded as the descendants of those unfortunate exiles, who were driven out of that kingdom in the religious wars. By others, they have been considered as descendants from the Jews expelled from Syria and Judæa under the Roman emperors. In short, every tradition concurs in representing them as having their origin in some persecution."

"But whatever this original stock must have been," said I, "it must doubtless have long since perished, even in its posterity. Their unsettled life is very unsuitable to keeping up their generation."

Mr. Younge suggested, that the species had been supported by subsequent additions; that it was a standing receptacle for all vagabonds and beggars: "but there is something in the true gipsey," said he, "which I cannot but consider as characteristic of a certain definite origin. They are all tall, raw-boned, and with raven locks; and though like the Jews of different countries they may have national traits, these traits are never sufficient to merge a certain essential character; they seem chiefly only minor differences added to others more strong and indelible."

We reached St. Laurence rather late, but were fortunate enough to procure a good supper, two fowls being killed for the purpose. The night, from some cause or other, was so chill, that we found it necessary to have a fire, and being in excellent spirits, we sate up late and talked merrily.

On the following morning we continued our progress. The scenery had so great a resemblance to the road of the preceding day, that I saw nothing worthy of detailed remark. The country was rich in views and in fertility. The agriculture, as far as I could judge of it, is very slovenly: the wheat is mowed, and gathered in by hand and in small carts. The labourers, however, appeared in tolerable good condition, and what cottages we passed by the road side, had every appearance of much comfort, and some substance. I must not forget to mention that I saw no cottage without a slip of land, and in many parts of the road, on the waste by its side, were single fruit trees railed round, which as I understood from Mr. Younge were the property of labourers, whose cottages were perhaps removed a league from their trees. These trees, which were in full bearing, are so much respected by the usage of the country, that they are never invaded. I was pleased with this trait of general honesty and confidence: it is common in America, but not in England.

We passed several chateaus in meadows and lawns by the road side: some of them were altogether in the ancient style, and so truly characteristic of the French country house, as to merit a more detailed description.

In the ordinary construction of a French chateau, there is a greater consumption of wood than brick, and no sparing of ground. It is usually a rambling building, with a body, wings, and again wings upon those wings; and flanked on each side with a pigeon-house, stables, and barns, the pigeon-house being on the right, and the barns and stables on the left. The decorations are infinitely beneath contempt; painted weathercocks and copper turrets, and even the paint apparently as ancient as the chateau. The windows are numerous, but even in the best chateaus there is strange neglect as to the broken glass; sometimes they are left as broken, but more frequently patched with paper, coloured silk, or even stuffed with linen. The upper tier of windows, even in the front of the house, is usually ornamented with the clothes of the family hanging out to dry, a piece of slovenliness and ill-taste for which there can assuredly be no excuse in the country where there is surely room enough for this part of household business. Upon the whole, the appearance of a French chateau, in the old style, resembles one of those deserted houses which are sometimes seen in England, where the plaister has been peeled or is peeling off, and where every boy that passes throws his stone at the windows.

The pleasure grounds attached to the chateau, very exactly correspond with its style: the chateau is usually built in the worst possible site of the whole estate. It generally stands in some meadow or lawn, and precisely in that part of it which is the natural drain of the whole, and where, if there were no house, there would necessarily be an horse-pond. A grand avenue, planted on each side with noble trees, leads up to the house, but is usually so overgrown with moss and weeds, as to convey a most uncomfortable feeling of cold, dampness, and desolation. The grass of the lawn is equally foul, and every thing of dirt and rubbish is collected under the windows in front. The gardens behind are in the same execrable state: gravel-walks over-run with moss and weeds; flower beds ornamented with statues of leaden Floras, painted Mercurys, and Dians with milk-pails. Every yard almost salutes you with some similar absurdity. The hedges are shaped into peacocks, and not unfrequently into ladies and gentlemen dancing a minuet. Pillars of cypress, and pyramids of yew, terminate almost every walk, and if there is an hollow in the garden, it is formed into a muddy pond, in which half a dozen nymphs in stone, are about to plunge. The ill-taste of these statues is not the worst; they are grossly indecent: nothing is reserved, nothing is concealed; and yet the master of the house will not hesitate to exhibit these to his female visitors, and what is worse, his female visitors will look at them with a pleasant smile. Once for all, there is no such thing as decency, as it is understood in other kingdoms, to be found in France. Nature is the fashion of the day, and according to the French philosophy, the passions are the best index to what is natural. With a very few exceptions, the French women act up to this doctrine, and are as natural as any one could wish them.

We passed through many pretty villages, and amongst them Clery, where Louis the Eleventh was buried. We visited the tomb of that memorable tyrant: it is of white marble, and the taste of it is good. The King is represented as kneeling, and in the attitude of addressing his prayers to the Virgin. The church of Clery was built by this King, and it was his express wish that he should be interred in it. The monument was raised by Louis the Thirteenth. It contains likewise the heart of Charles the Eighth, and the body of Charlotte of Savoy, the wife of Louis the Eleventh. This monument has been much defaced, the hatred of the tyrant extending to his remains.

Clery was formerly a place of pilgrimage for the devout of all Europe. There is an absurd story of a great bell in the church, which was said to toll of itself, whenever any one, being in danger of any mischief by sea or land, made a vow to the Holy Virgin, that if he escaped, he would make a pilgrimage to Clery. The tolling of the bell was the acceptance of the vow on the part of the Virgin. What a pity, that credulity should injure the cause of true religion!

We passed over the bridge of Mesmion, where Francis Duke of Guise was assassinated. There is an ancient abbey of the Order of St. Benedict in this village: The vineyards in this district were beautiful, and apparently fertile to a degree. They are said * * * *.

We reached Orleans to dinner, and whilst it was preparing had a walk round the town. The ladies reserved themselves for the promenade, as we intended to remain till the following morning.

Orleans has a very near resemblance to Tours, though the latter town is certainly better built, and preferable in situation; Orleans, however, is situated very beautifully. The country is uneven and diversified, and the fields have the air of pleasure grounds, except in the luxuriant wildness of the hedges, and the frequent intermixture of orchard and fruit trees. As seen from the road, the aspect of Orleans is extremely picturesque: it reminded me strongly of some towns I had seen in the interior of England.

The interior of the town does not altogether correspond with the beauty of the country in which it stands: some of the streets are narrow, the houses old, and most execrably built. The principal street is in no way inferior to that of Tours: it is terminated by a noble bridge, which has lately been repaired from the ruinous state in which it was left by the Chouans. The Grand Place is spacious, and has an air of magnificence. The cathedral is worth peculiar attention: the first stone of it was laid in the year 1287, but it was not finished till the year 1567. The party of the Huguenots, having seized Orleans, destroyed a considerable part of the cathedral; but Henry the Fourth, having visited the town, caused it to be rebuilt. The chapels surrounding the altar are wainscotted with oak, and the pannels are deeply cut into representations of the histories of the New Testament. The representation of our blessed Saviour on the cross, and the figures of St. John and others of the Apostles, are very masterly. They are the work of Baptiste Tubi, an Italian sculptor who sought refuge in France.

The two towers built at the western extremity by Louis the Fifteenth, are generally known and celebrated; by some they have been considered as too highly ornamented, but their effect is great. Perhaps the ornaments may indeed lose their own effect by being attached to a building which, by exciting stronger emotions, necessarily merges the less. The prospect from the summit of these towers exceeds all powers of description. The country seems one boundless garden covered with vineyards, the richness of which at this season of the year must be seen to be understood. No description can convey it with force to the imagination.

The Maid of Orleans, and the history of the times connected with her, are too well known to render any detail of interest;—suffice it therefore to say, that there are still several relics of her, and that her memory is still held in veneration. In the Hotel de Ville is a portrait of her at full length: her face is extremely beautiful, a long oval, and has an air of melancholy grandeur which appeals forcibly to the heart. She wears on her head a cap, or rather a bonnet, in which is a white plume; her hair is auburn, and flows loosely down her back. Her neck is ornamented with a necklace, surmounted by a small collar. Her dress is what is termed a Vandyke robe; it fits closely, and is scolloped round the neck, arms, and at the bottom. She holds a sword in her hand. This picture is confirmed by its resemblance to her figure in a monument in the main street. Charles the Seventh and the Maid of Orleans are here represented kneeling before the body of our Saviour, as it lies in the lap of the Virgin Mary. The King is bare-headed, his helmet lying by him. The Maid of Orleans is opposite to him, her eyes attentively fixed on Heaven. This monument was executed by the command of Charles the Seventh, in the year 1458, and is therefore most probably a correct representation both of the figure of the King himself and of the Maid of Orleans.

We attended the ladies in the evening to the promenade, or to the parade, as it has now become the fashion to call it, since France, and every thing in France, has taken a military turn. I was much pleased with the beauty of the ladies, and still more with a modesty and simple elegance in their dress, which I had not expected. But I have observed more than once, that the fashions of the capital have improved as they have travelled downwards into the provinces. They lose their excess, or what we should call in wine, their rawness and their freshness. The bosom which was naked in Paris has here at least some covering, and there is even some appearance of petticoats. The colours, as being adapted to the season, purple and straw, I thought elegant. There were two or three of the younger ladies in the dresses of bacchanals; they were certainly tasty, but they did not please me.

We left Orleans at an early hour on the following day. The scenery continued to improve as we advanced farther on the banks of the Loire. For several miles it was so highly cultivated, and so naturally beautiful, as to resemble a continued garden: the houses and chateaus became neater, and every thing had an air of sprightliness and gaiety, which might have animated even Despair itself. We observed that the fields were even infested with game; they rose in the stubbles as we passed along, and any one might have shot them from the road. Though there are no game-laws in France, there is a decency and moderation in the lower orders which answers the same purpose. No one presumes to shoot game except on land of which he is the proprietor or tenant.

I know not whether I have before remarked, that almost every chateau has a certain number of fish-ponds, and a certain quantity of woodland, and that these are considered as such necessary appendages, that an house is scarcely regarded as habitable without them. The table of a French gentleman is almost solely supplied from his land. Having a plenty of poultry, fish, and rabbits, he gives very little trouble to his butcher. Hence in many of the villages meat is not to be had, and even in large towns the supply bears a very small proportion to what would seem to be the natural demand of the population.

Of all the provinces of France, those which compose the department of the Loire are the richest, and best cultivated; and if any foreigner would wish to fix his residence in France, let it be on the banks of this river.—Fish, as I have said before, is cheap and plentiful, and fowls about one-fourth of the price in England. The climate, not so southerly as to be intolerably hot, nor so northerly as to be continually humid, is perhaps the most healthy and pleasant in the world—the sun shines day after day in a sky of etherial blue; the spring is relieved by frequent intervals of sun, and the summer by breezes. The evening, in loveliness and serenity, exceeds all powers of description. The windows may be left safely open during the night; and night after night have I laid in my bed, and watched the course of the moon ascending in the fretted vault. Society, moreover, in this part of the kingdom, is always within the reach of those who can afford to keep it, and the expences of the best company are very trifling. I have mentioned, I believe, that an establishment of two men servants, a gardener, three maids, a family of from four to six in number, and a carriage with two horses, might with great ease be kept in the French provinces on an annual income from 250*l.* to 300*l.* per annum.

One distinction of French and English visiting I must not omit. In England, if any one come from any distance to visit the family of a friend, he of course takes his dinner, and perhaps his supper, but is then expected to return home. Unless he is a brother or uncle, and not even always then, he must not expect to have a bed. To remain day after day for a week or a fortnight, would be considered as an outrage. On the other hand, in France, a family no sooner comes to its chateau for the summer (for since the Revolution this has become the fashion), than preparation is immediately made for parties of visitors. Every day brings some one, who is never suffered to go, as long as he can be detained. Every chateau thus becomes a pleasant assemblage, and in riding, walking, and fishing, nothing can pass more agreeably than a French summer in the country. As we passed along, we met several of these parties in their morning rides; they invariably addressed us, and very frequently invited us to their houses, though perfectly strangers to us. The mode of living in these country residences differs very little from what is common in the same rank of life in England. The breakfast consists of tea, coffee, fruits, and cold meat. The dinner is usually at two o'clock, and is served up as in England. The French however have not as yet imitated the English habit of sitting at table. Coffee in a saloon or pavilion, fronting the garden and lawn, immediately follows the dinner: this consumes about two hours. The company then divide into parties, and walk. They return about eight o'clock to tea. After tea they dance till supper. Supper is all gaiety and gallantry, and the latter perhaps of a kind, which in England would not be deemed very innocent. The champagne then goes round, and the ladies drink as much as the gentlemen, that is to say, enough to exhilarate, not to overwhelm the animal spirits. A French woman with three or four glasses of wine in her head, would certainly make an English one stare; but France is the land of love, and it is an universal maxim that life is insipid without it.

We slept in a village, of which I have not noted the name: the ladies, as usual, were huddled in one room, and Mr. Younge, as usual, was not excluded from their party. For my own part I can sleep any where, and I slept this night in the kitchen. The landlord, from civility, insisted on having the honour of sleeping in the opposite corner. I very willingly acceded to his request, and having made up a cheerful fire, we composed ourselves in two chairs. The landlady seemed very indignant that her husband should desert her bed: she was sure that Monsieur was not afraid of remaining by himself. Her husband, she added, had a rheumatism, and the night air might injure him. I was resolved, however, for once to do mischief, or perhaps to do good, so said nothing, and the husband was accordingly obliged to abide by his offer, and remain in the kitchen.

### CHAP. XVI.

*Comparative Estimate of French and English Country Inns—Tremendous Hail Storm—Country Masquerade—La Charité—Beauty and Luxuriance of its Environs—Nevers—Fille-de-Chambre—Lovely Country between Nevers and Moulins—Treading Corn—Moulins—Price of Provisions.*

WE were two more days on our journey to La Charité: the scenery continued the same, except that the surface became more level. On both sides of the Loire, however, there was that appearance of plenty and of happiness, of the bounty of Nature and of the cheerful labour of man, which inspirits the heart of the beholder. The painters have very justly adopted it as a maxim, that no landscape is perfect, in which there are not the appendages of life and motion. The truth is, that man, as a being formed for society, is never so much interested as by man, and it is hence a maxim of feeling, as well as of moral duty, that nothing is foreign to him as an individual which is connected with him in nature.

In this part of our journey we saw more of French inns of all degrees than we had hitherto experienced. I believe I have already mentioned, that a very wrong idea prevails as to their comparative merit. In substantial provision and accommodation, the French inns are not a whit inferior to English of the same degree; but they are inferior to them in all the minor appendages. In point of eating and drinking the French inns infinitely exceed the English: their provisions are of a better kind, and are much cheaper: we scarcely slept any where, where we could not procure fowls of all kinds, eggs and wine. It is too true, indeed, that their mode of cooking is not very well suited to an English palate; but a very little trouble will remedy this inconvenience. The French cooks are infinitely obliging in this respect—they will take your instructions, and thank you for the honor done them. The dinner, moreover, when served up, will consist of an infinite variety, and that without materially swelling the bill. Add to this the dessert, of which an English inn-keeper, except in the most expensive hotels, has not a single idea. In France, on the other hand, in the poorest inns, in the most ordinary hedge ale-house, you will have a dessert of every fruit in season, and always tastily and even elegantly served. The wine, likewise, is infinitely better than what is met with on the roads in England. In the article of beds, with a very few exceptions, the French inns exceed the English: if a traveller carry his sheets with him, he is always secure of an excellent hair mattrass, or if he prefer it, a clean feather-bed. On the other side, the French inns are certainly inferior to the English in their apartments. The bed-room is too often the dining-room. The walls are merely whitewashed, or covered with some execrable pictures. There are no such things as curtains, or at least they are never considered as necessary. There is neither soap, water, nor towel, to cleanse yourself when you rise in the morning. A Frenchman has no idea of washing himself before he breakfasts. The furniture, also, is always in the worst possible condition. We were often puzzled to contrive a tolerable table: the one in most common use is composed of planks laid across two stools or benches. The chairs are usually of oak, with perpendicular backs. There are no bells; and the attendants are more frequently male than female, though this practice is gradually going out of vogue. There is a great change moreover, of late years, in the civility of the landlords— they will now acknowledge their obligations to you, and not, as formerly, treat you as intruders.

To sum up the comparison between a French and English provincial inn, the expences for the same kind of treatment, allowing only for the necessary national differences, are about one-fourth of what they would be in England. In the course of our tour, we were repeatedly detained for days together at some of the inns on the road, and our whole suite, amounting to seven in number, never cost us more than at the rate of an English guinea a day. In England I am confident it would have been four times the sum.

The last post but one before we reached La Charité, we were overtaken by a tremendous shower of hail, a calamity, for such it is, which too frequently afflicts this part of France. The hail-tones were at least as large as nuts: some trees were at hand, under which we drove for shelter. Had we been in an open exposed road, I have no doubt but that the horses must have been hurt. I was informed, that these storms are sometimes so violent as to kill the lambs, and even to wound in a very dangerous manner the larger cattle. They usually happen about the end of the spring and the summer.

We passed some very pretty peasant girls, dressed in bodices laced crossways with ribbon. They informed us that they were the daughters of a small farmer, and were going to a neighbouring chateau to dance at the birth-day of one of the ladies of the family. Mr. Younge complimented them on their beauty; they smiled with more grace than seemed to belong to their station. Our ladies at this instant came up; the young peasants made a curtsey, which instantly betrayed their secret to Mrs. Younge and Mademoiselle St. Sillery. "Where is the masque?" said the latter. "In the Chateau de Thiery," replied one of them, "about a fourth part of a league through this gateway; perhaps, if you are going only to the next post, you will join us. Papa and Mamma will be honored by your company." The invitation was declined with many thanks to the charming girls. It is needless to add, that they were young ladies habited as peasants, and that there was a masque at the chateau. This kind of entertainment is very common in this part of France.

We reached La Charité in such good time, that we resolved to push on for Nevers. I had a walk round the town whilst our coffee was preparing. The interior of the town does not merit a word; the streets are narrow, the houses low and dark, and this too in a country where the Loire rolls its beautiful stream through meadows and plains, and where ground is plentiful and cheap. I can readily account for the narrow streets in capital cities, where locality has an artificial value, and where the competition is necessarily great. But whence are the streets thus huddled together, and the air thus carefully excluded, where there is no such want of ground or value of building lots? It must here originate purely in that execrable taste which characterized the early ages.

The environs of the town, the fields, the meadows, the gently rising hills, and the recluse vallies, compensate for the vile interior: Nature here reigns in all her loveliness, and a poet, a painter, even any one of ordinary feeling, could not see her without delight and admiration. There are innumerable nightingales in the woods at a small distance from the town. If the French noblesse had the taste of the English, the vicinity of La Charité would be covered with villas.

We took our coffee on a kind of raised mound, at the extremity of a garden, which overhung the Loire. A lofty and spreading tree overshadowed us, and stretched its branches over the river. In the fork, formed where the trunk first divides into the greater branches, was a railed seat and table. The view from hence over the meadow on the opposite bank, was gay and picturesque. The peasant girls were milking their cows and singing with their usual merriment. Parties of the townsmen were playing at golf; others were romping, running, walking, with all the thoughtless erility of the French character. I never enjoyed an hour more sensibly. The evening was delightful, and all around seemed gay and happy.

Our journey to Nevers was partly by moon-light. The road exceeds all powers of description. It was frequently bordered by hedges of flowering shrubs, and such cottages as we passed seemed sufficient for the climate. Why might not Marmontel have lived in such a cottage? thought I, as I rode by more than one of them. This spot of France certainly excells every part of the world. Even the clay and chalk-pits are verdant: the sides are covered with shrubs which are raised with difficulty even in the hot-houses of England.

Our inn at Nevers, the Grand Napoleon, had nothing to correspond with its sounding title; our bed-chambers, however, were pleasantly situated, and for once since we had left Orleans, we had each of us his own apartment. The fille-de-chambre too was handsome and cleanly-looking, but somewhat more loquacious than a weary traveller required. She endeavoured to bring me into a conversation on the subject of Mademoiselle St. Sillery's beauty. The familiar impertinence of these girls must be seen to be understood. One maxim is universal in France—that difference of rank has no place between a man and a woman. A fille-de-chambre is on a perfect footing of equality with a marshal of France, and will address, and converse with him as such. They enter your room without knocking, stay as long as they like, and will remain whilst you are undressing. If you exhibit any modest unwillingness, they laugh at you, and perhaps two or three of them will come in to rally Monsieur. I must do them the justice, however, to add, that though their raillery will be sometimes broad enough, it is never verbally indelicate. There is less of this in the lower ranks in France than in England. The decencies are observed in word, however violated in fact.

Nevers is a pleasant town, and very agreeably situated on the declivities of an hill, at the bottom of which flows the Loire. On the summit of the hill is what remains of the palace of the ancient Counts; it has of course suffered much from time, but enough still remains to bear testimony to its original magnificence. We visited some of the apartments. The tapestry, though nearly three centuries old, still retains in a great degree the original brilliancy of its colours: the figures are monstrous, but the general effect is magnificent. There is a portrait of Madame de Montespan, the second acknowledged mistress of Louis the Fourteenth. According to the fashion of the age, her hair floats down her shoulders. She is habited in a loose robe, and has one leg half naked. Her face has the French character; it is long, but beautiful: its principal expression seemed to me voluptuousness, with something of the haughty beauty. It is well known that her temper was violent in the extreme, and perhaps the knowledge of this circumstance might have impressed me with an idea which I have imputed to the expression of the picture.

The cathedral of Nevers is one of the most ancient in France. About one hundred years since, in digging a vault, a body was discovered enveloped in a long robe; some very old coins were found in the coffin, and the habit in which the body was wrapped was of itself of the most ancient fashion. According to the French antiquaries, this was the body of one of the ancient dukes of Nevers. There are many other antiquities in the town, but I do not find that I have noted them, except that they exist in sufficient numbers to establish the ancient origin of this capital of the Nivernois.

Nothing can be more picturesque than the country between Nevers and Moulins. Natural beauty, and the life and activity of cultivation, unite to render it the most complete succession of landscape in France. The road is gravel, and excellent to a degree. It is bordered by magnificent trees, but which have been so planted, as to procure shade without excluding air; the road, therefore, is at once shady and dry. The chesnut trees, which are numerous in this part of the Bourbonnois, in beauty at least, infinitely exceed the British oaks: they have a bossy foliage, which reminds one of the Corinthian volutes. The French peasantry are not insensible of this beauty—wherever there was a tree of this kind of more than common luxuriance in its foliage, a seat was made around the trunk, and the turf mowed and ornamented, so as to shew that it was the scene of the village sports. Though England has many delightful villages, and rustic greens, France beats it hollow in rural scenery; and I believe I have before mentioned, that the French peasantry equally exceed the English peasantry in the taste and rustic elegance with which they ornament their little domains. On the great scale, perhaps, taste is better understood in England than in France, but as far as Nature leads, the sensibility of the French peasant gives him the advantage. Some of the gardens in the provinces of France are delightful.

We passed several fields in which the farming labourers were treading out their corn; indeed the country all around was one universal scene of gaiety and activity in the exercise of this labour. The manner in which it is done is, I believe, peculiar to France. Three or four layers of corn, wheat, barley, or pease, are laid upon some dry part of the field, generally under the central tree; the horses and mules are then driven upon it and round it in all directions, a woman being in the centre like a pivot, and holding the reins: the horses are driven by little girls. The corn thrashed out is cleared away by the men, others winnow it, others heap it, others supply fresh layers. Every one seems happy and noisy, the women and girls singing, the men occasionally resting from their labour to pay their gallant attentions. The scene is so animated as to inspirit the beholder. It is evident, however, that this cheap method of getting up their harvest, is only practicable in countries where the climate is settled: even in this province they are sometimes surprised with a shower, but as the sun immediately bursts out with renewed fervour, every thing is soon put to rights. In Languedoc, as I understood, they have no barns whatever, and therefore this practice is universal. The wheat was not very heavy, it resembled barley rather than wheat; the average crop about sixteen English bushels. Nothing is so vexatious as the French measures; I do not understand them yet, though I have inquired of every one.

Moulins somewhat disappointed my expectation. It is indeed, beautifully situated, in the midst of a rising and variegated country, with meadows, corn-fields, hills, and woods, to which may be added the river Allier, a stream so recluse and pretty, and so bordered with beautiful grounds, as to give the idea of a park. These grounds, moreover, are laid out as if for the pleasure of the inhabitants: the meadows and corn-fields are intersected by paths in every direction; and fruit-trees are in great number, and to all appearance are common property. There is something very interesting in these characteristics of simple benevolence; they recall the idea of the primæval ages. I have an indistinct memory of a beautiful passage in Ovid, which describes the Golden Age. I am writing, however, without the aid or presence of books, and therefore must refer the classical reader to the original.

The interior of the town does not merit description: the streets are narrow, the houses dark, and built in the worst possible style. The architect has carried the idea of a city into the country: there is the same economy of ground and light, and the same efforts for huddling and comprehending as much brick and mortar as possible in the least possible space. Its origin was in the fourteenth century. The Dukes of Bourbon selected it as a place of residence during the season of the chace, and having built a castle in the neighbourhood, their suite and descendants shortly founded a town. This, indeed, was the usual origin of most of the provincial towns in Europe; they followed the castle or the chateau of the Baron. As seen in the fields and meadows in the vicinity of the town, Moulins has a very agreeable appearance. The river, and the beautiful scenery around it, compensate for its disagreeable interior; and some trees being intermixed with the buildings of the town give an air of gaiety and the picturesque to the town itself.

The market-place is only worthy of mention as introducing the price of provisions. Moulins is as cheap as Tours: beef, and mutton, and veal, are plentiful; vegetables scarcely cost any thing, and fuel is very moderate. Fruit is so cheap as scarcely to be sold, and very good; eggs two dozen for an English sixpence; poultry abundant, and about sixpence a fowl. A good house, such a one as is usually inhabited by the lawyer, the apothecary, or a gentleman of five or six hundred per annum, in the country towns in England, is at Moulins from twelve to fourteen pounds per year, including garden and paddock.

Our inn at Moulins, however, was horrible: our beds would have frightened any one but an experienced traveller.

### CHAP. XVII.

*Country between Moulins and Rouane—Bresle—Account of the Provinces of the Nivernois and Bourbonnois—Climate—Face of the Country—Soil—Natural Produce—Agricultural Produce—Kitchen Garden—French Yeomen—Landlords—Price of Land—Leases—General Character of the French Provincial Farmers.*

ON the following day we left Moulins for Lyons. The distance between the two places exceeds an hundred miles; we distributed, therefore, our journey into three days, making Rouane on the Loire, and Bresle, our intermediate sleeping places.

Between Moulins and Rouane, that is to say, during the whole of our first day's journey, the country is a succession of hills and valleys, of open and inclosed, of fields and of woodland, which render it to the eyes of a northern traveller the most lovely country in the world. In proportion, however, as the country becomes more fertile, the roads become worse. We had got now into roads comparatively very bad, but still not so bad as in England and America. The beauty of the scenery, however, compensated for this defect of the roads. We met many waggons, the hind wheels of which were higher than those in front. This is one of the few things in which the French farmers exhibit more knowledge than the English. These wheels of the waggons were shod with wood instead of iron. We passed several vineyards, in which the vines were trained by maples, and festooned from tree to tree. They looked fanciful and picturesque. The vines of this country, however, are said to yield better in quantity than in quality. They produce much, but the wine is bad, and not fit for exportation.

In every hedge we passed were medlars, plumbs, cherries, and maples with vines trained to them. This abundance of fruit gives an air of great plenty, and likewise much improves the beauty of the country. The French fruit of almost every kind exceeds the English. An exception must be made with respect to apples, which are better in England than in any country in the world. But the grapes, the plumbs, the pears, the peaches, the nectarines, and the cherries of France, have not their equal all the world over. They are of course cheap in proportion to their abundance. The health of the peasantry may perhaps in good part be imputed to this vegetable abundance. It is a constant maxim with physicians, that those countries are most healthy, where from an ordinary laxative diet, the body is always kept open. Half the diseases in the world originate in obstructions.

Rouane is a considerable town on the Loire; it is very ancient in its origin, and its appearance corresponds with its antiquity. It is chiefly used as an entrepôt for all the merchandize, corn, wine, &c. which is sent down the Loire. It is accordingly a place of infinite bustle, and in despite of the river, is very dirty. He must be more fastidious than belongs to a traveller, who cannot excuse this necessary appendage of trade, and particularly in a town on the Loire, where a walk of ten minutes will carry him from the narrow streets into one of the sweetest countries under Heaven. Even the necessary filth of commerce cannot destroy, or scarcely deface the beauty of the country.

Our inn at Rouane was execrable beyond measure. Without any regard to decency, we were introduced into a sleeping room with three beds, and informed that Monsieur and Madame Younge were to sleep in one, Mademoiselle St. Sillery in another, and myself in the third. It was not without difficulty that I could procure another arrangement. The beds, moreover, were without pillows.

From Rouane to Bresle the country assumes a mountainous form, and the road is bordered with chesnut trees. We had got now into the district of mulberries, and we passed innumerable trees of them. Like other fruit-trees, they grow wild, in the middle of fields, hedge-rows, and by the road side. A stranger travelling in France is led to conclude, that there is no such thing as property in fruit. Every one may certainly gather as much as he chuses for his own immediate use. The peasants of this part of the province are land proprietors; some of them possess twelve or fourteen acres, others an hill, others a garden or a single field. They appeared poor but comfortable. They raise a great quantity of poultry and pigs, and reminded me very forcibly of the Negroes in the West India Islands—a hard-working, happy, and cheerful race. I should not, perhaps, omit to mention, that the houses of the peasants were very different from any that I had yet seen. For the most part, they are square, white, and with flat roofs. They are almost totally without glass in the windows; but the climate is generally so dry and delightful, that glass perhaps would rather be an annoyance. We are apt to attach ideas of comfort or misery according to circumstances peculiarly belonging to ourselves. Tell an English peasant that a Frenchman has neither glass to his windows, nor sheets to his bed, and he will conclude him to be miserable in the extreme. On the other hand, tell a French peasant, that an English rustic never tastes a glass of wine once in seven years, and he will equally pity the Englishman.

Bresle is one of those villages which impress a traveller with a strong idea of the beauty of the country, and of the state of the comfort of its inhabitants. It is broad, clean, and most charmingly situated. On every side of it rises a wall of mountains, covered to their very summits with vines, and interspersed with the cottages of the Vignerons. The river Tardine flows through the valley. This is what is termed a mountain river, being in summer a brook, and in winter a torrent. In the year 1715 it rose so high as to sweep away half the town: the inhabitants were surprised in their beds, and many of them were drowned. The river, when we passed, had no appearance of being capable of this tremendous force: it resembled a little brook, in which a shallow stream of very transparent water rolled over a bed of gravel. "How happy might an hermit be," said Mademoiselle St. Sillery, "in a cottage on the side of one of those hills! There is a wood for him to walk in, and a brook to encourage him, by its soft murmurs, to sleep." I agreed in the observation which exactly characterizes the scenery.

Our inn at this town was in the midst of a garden, covered with fruits and flowers. Our beds reminded me of England, except that again there were no pillows, and absolutely nothing in the chamber but a bed. Every thing, however, was delightfully clean; and as I lay in my bed, I was serenaded by a nightingale.

The road between Moulins and Lyons is certainly the most picturesque part of France; every league presented me with something to admire, and to note. My observations were accordingly so numerous, that I have deemed it necessary to arrange them in some form, and to present them in a kind of connected picture. Mr. Younge had the kindness to answer all my questions as far as his own knowledge went; and where he was at a loss himself, seized the first opportunity of inquiry from others. In France, this is more practicable than it would be in any other country. The French of all classes, as I have repeatedly had occasion to observe, are unwearied in their acts of kindness; they offer their minor services with sincerity, and you cannot oblige them more than by accepting them, nor disappoint them more than by declining them. They have nothing of the surliness of the Englishman. It would be considered as the most savage brutality to hesitate in, and more particularly to refuse with rudeness, any possible satisfaction to a stranger. To be a stranger is to be a visitor, and to be a visitor is to have a claim to the most extreme hospitality and attention. I can never enough praise the French people for their indiscriminate, their natural, their totally uninterested and spontaneous benevolence.

I wish to convey a clear idea of this garden of France: I shall therefore give my observations in full under the heads of, its climate, its produce, its agriculture, and the manners of its provincial inhabitants.

The climate of the departments of the Nievre and the Allier, which include the provinces of the Nivernois and Bourbonnois, is the most delightful under Heaven, being at once most healthy, and such as to animate and inspirit the senses and the imagination: it is an endless succession of the most lovely skins, without any interruption, except by those rains which are necessary to nourish and fertilize. The winters are mild, without fogs, and with sufficient sunshine to render fires almost unnecessary. The springs answer to the ordinary weather of May in other kingdoms. The summer and autumn—with the exception of hail and thunder, which are certainly violent, but not frequent—are not characterized by those heavy humid heats, which are so pestilential in some parts of South America: they are light, elastic, and cheering. The windows of the bed-chambers, as I have before mentioned, are almost all without glass; or, if they have them, it is for show rather than for use: the universal custom is, to sleep with them open. It is nothing uncommon to have the swallows flying into your chamber, and awakening you by early dawn with their twittering. When these windows open into gardens, nothing can be more pleasant: the purity of the air, the splendor of the stars, the singing of nightingales, and the perfume of flowers, all concur to charm the senses; and I never remember to have enjoyed sweeter slumbers, and pleasanter hours, than whilst in this part of France.

In March and April, the ground is covered with flowers; and many which are solely confined to the gardens and hot-houses in England, may be seen in the fields and hedge-rows. The colours are perhaps not altogether so brilliant as in more humid climates, but be they what they may, they, give the country an appearance of a fairy land. Pease are in common use on every table in March, and every kind of culinary vegetable is equally forward. The meadows are covered with violets, and the gardens with roses: the banks by the side of the road seem one continued bed of cowslips. In plain words, Spring here indeed seems to hold her throne, and to reign in all that vernal sweetness and loveliness which is imputed to her by the poets.

The health of the inhabitants corresponds with the excellence of the climate. Gouts, rheumatisms, and even colds, are very rare, and fevers not frequent. The most common complaint is a dysentery, towards the latter end of the autumn.

The face of the country throughout the two departments of the Nievre and the Allier, is what has been above described—an uninterrupted succession of rich landscape, in which every thing is united which constitutes the picturesque. The country sometimes rises into hills, and even mountains; none of which are so barren but to have vineyards, or gardens, to their very summits. In many of them, where the surface is common property, the peasantry, in order to make the most of its superficial area, have dug it into terraces, on which each of them has his vineyard, or garden for herbs, corn, and fruits. The industry of the French peasantry is not exceeded in any part of the world: wherever they possess a spot of land, they improve it to its utmost possible capacity. Under this careful cultivation, there is in reality no such thing in France as a sterile mountain. If there be no natural soil, they will carry some thither.

There are numerous woods and forests in these departments. The wood being interspersed amongst the hills and valleys, contribute much to the beauty of the scenery: the same circumstance contributes more, perhaps, to the comfort of the inhabitants. Fuel, so dear in almost every other part of France, is here cheap to an extraordinary degree. Coal is likewise found at some depth from the surface; but, of course, no use is made of it. The French woods are more luxuriant, and generally composed of more beautiful trees than those in England and in America. The chesnut-tree, so common in France, is perhaps unrivalled in its richness of foliage. The underwood, moreover, is less ragged and troublesome. Nothing can be more delightful than an evening walk in a French wood.

The soil of the department of the Allier is rather light: on the hills it is calcareous; in the vales it is a white calcareous loam, the surface of which is a most fertilizing manure of marl and clay. The hills, therefore, are peculiarly adapted for vines, which they produce in great quantities; and when on favourable sites, that is to say, with respect to the sun, the quality of the wine corresponds with the quantity. In this province, perhaps, there is a less proportion of waste land than in any other department in France. The people are industrious, and the soil is fruitful. There are certainly some wastes, which, under proper cultivation, might be rendered fertile. I passed over many of these, when an idea naturally arose in my mind, what a different appearance they would assume under English or American management. But the bad management of the French farmers is no derogation from the just praise of its rich soil.

The natural and agricultural produce is such, as to render these provinces worthy of their characteristic designation—they are truly the garden of France. The most beautiful shrubs are common in the woods and hedges: not a month in the year but one or other of them are in full flower and foliage. The botanist might be weary before he had concluded his task. To a northern traveller, nothing appears more astonishing than the garden-like air of the fields in France: he will see in the woods and forests, what he has been hitherto accustomed to see only in hot-houses. The natural history of these provinces would be an inexhaustible subject: the cursory traveller can only describe generally.

Wheat, barley, oats, grasses, roots, and vines, are the staple agricultural produce. The wheat is certainly not so heavy as that in England, but the barley is not inferior to any barley in the world. The French farmers calculate upon reaping about sevenfold; if they sow one bushel, they reap, between six and seven. Potatoes have likewise, of late years, become an article of field-culture and general consumption in every department of France, and particularly in those of the Loire, the Allier, and the Nievre. Every city is supplied with them almost in as much abundance as the cities of England and America. Where wheat is scarce, the peasantry substitute them as bread. To say all in a word, they have of late years got into general consumption; though before the Revolution they were scarcely known.

The kitchen-garden in the French provinces is by no means so contemptible as it has been described by some travellers. In this respect they have done the French great injustice. I will venture to assert, on the other hand, that nothing is cultivated in the kitchen-gardens of England and America, but what, either by the aid of a better climate, or of more careful and assiduous culture, is brought to more perfection, and produced in greater plenty, in the kitchen-gardens of France. I have already mentioned potatoes, which are cultivated both in the garden and in the field: artichokes and asparagus are in great plenty, and comparatively most surprisingly cheap—as many may be bought for a penny in France as for a shilling in England. The environs of Lyons are celebrated for their excellent artichokes; they are carefully conveyed in great quantities to the tables of the rich all over the kingdom. Pease, beans, turnips, carrots, and onions, are equally plentifully cultivated, equally good, and equally cheap.

I have frequently had occasion to speak of the slovenly agriculture of the French farmers, and I am sorry to have to add, that the fertility of the provinces of Nivernois and the Bourbonnois, is rather to be imputed to the felicity of their soil and climate than to their cultivation. There is certainly a vast proportion of waste land in these provinces, which only remains waste, because the French landlords and farmers want the knowledge to bring it into cultivation. Many hundreds of acres are let at about twelve sols (sixpence) per acre, and would be sold at about a Louis d'or, which in three years, under English management, would be richly worth thirty pounds. What a country would this be to purchase in, if with himself an Englishman or an American could transport his own labourers and ideas. But nothing is to be done without assistance.

Many of the French landlords retain a great portion of their estates in their own hands, and cultivate it with more knowledge and with more liberality than their farmers. A gentleman, farming his own lands, is always useful to the country, if not to himself. He may improve his lands beyond their worth—he may ruin himself, therefore, but the country is proportionately benefitted by having so many good acres where it had before so many bad. Some of the restored Emigrants have most peculiarly benefitted France, by bringing into it English improvements. I have more than once had occasion to remark, that this change is visible in many parts of the kingdom, and will produce in time still more important effects.

The price of land is by two-thirds cheaper than in England, I am speaking now of the Nivernois and Bourboranois. It is generally about eighteen or twenty years purchase of the rent. If the rent be about 300l. English for about five hundred acres of land—half arable, a fourth forest, and a fourth waste—the purchase will be about 5500 guineas. The very same estate in any part of England would be about 15,000. But in England the forest and waste would be brought into cultivation. The forest is here little better than a waste, and the waste is turned to as little purpose as if it were the wild sea beach.

The farms in the Nivernois are very small; the farmers are by natural consequence poor. They have neither the spirit nor the means of improvement. They are in fact but a richer kind of peasantry. Those writers have surely never lived in the country, who urge the national utility of small farms. The immediate consequences of small farms are an overflow of population, and such a division and sub-division of sustenance, as to reduce the poor to the lowest possible point of sustenance. Population, within certain limits, may doubtless constitute the strength of a nation; but who will contend, that a nation of beggars, a nation overflowing with a starved miserable superfluity, is in a condition of enviable strength?

There are few or no leases in these provinces, and this is doubtless one of the reasons why agriculture has remained where it now is for these four or five last centuries. The common course of the crops is wheat, barley, fallow; or beans, barley, and wheat, and fallow. In some of the provinces, it is wheat, fallow, and wheat, fallow, in endless succession.

I do not understand enough of the vine culture to give any opinion as to the French vineyards, but by all that I have observed, I must fully assent to the generally received opinion, that the vine is better understood in France than in Portugal, and that wines are, in fact, the natural staple in France. It is the peculiar excellence of the vine, that it does not require fertile land. It will most flourish where nothing but itself will take root. How happy therefore is it for France, that she can thus turn her barrens into this most productive culture, and make her mountains, as it were, smile.

If an Englishman or an American were inclined to give a trial to a settlement in France, I would certainly advise them to fix on one of these central departments. They will find a soil and climate such as I have described, and which I think has not its equal in the world. They will find land cheap; and as it may be improved, and even the cheap price is rated according to its present rent, they will find this cheapness to be actually ten times as cheap as it appears. They will find, moreover, cheerful neighbours, a people polished in their manners from the lowest to the highest, and naturally gay and benevolent.

## CHAP. XVIII.

*Lyons—Town-Hall-Hotel de Dieu—Manufactories—Price of Provisions—State of Society—Hospitality to Strangers—Manners—Mode of Living—Departure— Vienne—French Lovers.*

WE reached Lyons in the evening of the third day after we left Moulins. We remained there two days, and employed nearly the whole of the time in walks over the city and environs. I adopted this practice as the invariable rule on the whole course of my tour—to have certain points where we might repose, and thence take a view both of the place itself, and a retrospect of what we had passed.

Nothing can be more delightful to the eye than the situation of Lyons. Situated on the confluence of two of the most lovely rivers in the world, the Rhone and the Saone, and distributed, as it were, on hills and dales, with lawn, corn-fields, woods and vineyards interposed, and gardens, trees, &c. intermixed with the houses, it has a liveliness, an animation, an air of cleanness, and rurality, which seldom belong to a populous city. The distant Alps, moreover, rising in the back ground, add magnificence to beauty. Beyond all possibility of doubt, Lyons is unrivalled in the loveliness of its situation. The approach to it is like the avenue to fairy-land.

The horrible ravage of the Revolution has much defaced this town. La Place de Belle Cour was once the finest square which any provincial town in Europe could boast. It was composed of the most magnificent houses, the habitations of such of the nobility as were accustomed to make Lyons their winter or summer residence. That demon, in the human shape, Collot d'Herbois, being sent to Lyons as one of the Jacobin Commissioners, by one and the same decree condemned the houses to be razed to the ground, and their possessors to be guillotined. A century will pass before Lyons will recover itself from this Jacobin purgation. In this square was formerly an equestrian statue of Louis the Fourteenth, adorned on the sides of the pedestal with bronze figures of the Rhone and the Saone. This statue is destroyed, but the bronze figures remain.

The town-hall of Lyons is in every respect worthy of the city. It is in the form of a parallelogram, with wings on each side of the front, each wing being nearly one hundred and fifty yards in length. The middle of the wings are crowned with cupolas, and the gates have all Ionic pillars. The walls and ceilings are covered with paintings. There are several inscriptions in honour of the Emperor Napoleon; but as these have been already noted in other books of travels, I deem it unnecessary to say more of them. But the best praise of Lyons is in its institutions for charity, in its hospitals, and in its schools. In no city in the world have they so great a proportion to the actual population and magnitude of the town. They are equal to the support of one eighth part of the inhabitants. The Hotel Dieu is in fact a palace built for the sick poor. The rooms are lofty, with cupolas, and all of them very carefully ventilated. The beds are clean to an extreme degree, as was likewise every utensil in the kitchen, and the kitchen itself. The nursing, feeding, &c. of the sick is performed by a religious society of about one hundred men, and the same number of women, who devote themselves to that purpose. The men are habited in black; the women in the dress of nuns. This charity is open to all nations; to be an admissible object, nothing further is necessary than to stand in need of its assistance. This is true charity.

The cathedral is beautifully situated by the river: it is dedicated to St. John, and is built in the ancient Gothic style. The clock is a great favourite with the inhabitants. It is ornamented by a cock, which is contrived so as to crow every hour. Before the Revolution, the church of Lyons was the richest in France, or Europe. All the canons were counts, and were not admissible, till they had proved sixteen quarters of nobility. They wore a gold cross of eight rays. Since the Revolution, the cathedral has fallen into decay; but it is to be hoped that, for the honour of the town, it will be repaired.

Lyons has two theatres, Le Grand, and Le Petit Spectacle. Neither of them deserve any more than a bare mention. The performers had so little reputation, that we had no wish to visit either of them.

The manufactories of Lyons, being confined in their supply to the home market, are not in the same flourishing state as formerly. They still continue, however, to work up a vast quantity of silk, and on the return of peace, would doubtless recover somewhat of their former prosperity. Some years since, the silk stockings alone worked up at Lyons, were estimated at 1500 pair daily. The workmen are unhappily not paid in proportion to their industry. They commence their day's labour at an unusual hour in the morning, and continue it in the night, yet are unable to earn enough to live in plenty.

Lyons appeared to me, from the cursory information which I could obtain, to be as cheap as any town in France. Provisions of all kinds were in great plenty, and were the best of their kind. There are three kinds of bread—the white bread, meal bread, and black or rye bread. The latter is in most use amongst the weavers. It is very cheap, but the measures differ so much in this part of France, that I could not reduce them to English pounds, except by a rough estimate. The best wheaten bread is about one-third or rather more of the price that it is in England; beef and mutton in great plenty, and proportionately cheap; a very large turkey for about two shillings and sixpence, English money. Pit coal is in common use in almost every house in Lyons: it is dug in the immediate neighbourhood, and is very cheap. The best land in the province may be had for about fifteen pounds (English) per acre in purchase. In the neighbourhood of Lyons, the land lets high, and therefore sells proportionately. Vegetables are of course in the greatest possible plenty, and fruit so cheap and so abundant, as to be sold only by the poorest people. Whoever is particularly fond of a dessert, let him seek it in France: for a livre he may set out a table, which in London would take him at least a Louis.

Lyons has given birth to many celebrated men. Amongst them was De Lanzy, the celebrated mathematician, and friend of Maupertuis. He lived to such an extreme age as to survive his memory and faculties; but when so insensible as to know no one about him, Maupertuis suddenly asked him what was the square of 12, and he readily replied, 144, and died, as it is said, almost in the same moment. This illustrious genius was as simple as he was learned. His character, as given amongst the history of the French literati, is very amiable— of great learning, of extreme industry, simple and amiable to a degree, and invariably benevolent and good-tempered. He was yet more distinguished by his charities than by his learning. The learned Thon likewise was a native of this town.

The society at Lyons very much resembles that of Paris; it is divided into two classes—those in trade, *i. e.* merchants, and those out of trade; the military, gentry, &c. The military, though many of them are certainly of rather an humble origin, are characterized by elegant manners, by great politeness, and by a gallantry towards the ladies which would have done honour to the old court. It gave me great satisfaction to hear this character of them. I should put no value on any society in which the ladies did not hold their due place and perform their due parts, and this is never the case, except where they are properly respected. Gallantry has the same effect upon the manners which Ovid attributes to learning—"*Emollit mores nec sinit esse feros.*"

A stranger at Lyons, who makes the city his temporary residence, is received with the greatest hospitality into all the parties of the town; he requires nothing but an introduction to one of them; and even if he should be without that, an unequivocal appearance of respectability would answer the same end. The fashionable world at Lyons, however, are not accustomed to give dinners; they have no notion of that substantial hospitality which characterizes England. Their suppers however are very elegant: they have always fish, and sometimes soup, roasted poultry, and in the proper season, game—pease, cauliflowers, and asparagus, almost the whole year round. The sparkling Champagne then goes round, and French wit, French vivacity, and French gallantry, are seen in perfection. There is certainly nothing in England equal to the French supper. It is usually served in a saloon, but the company make no hesitation, in the intervals of conversation and of eating, to visit every room in the house. Every room is accordingly lighted and prepared for this purpose; the beds thrust into cupboards and corners, and the whole house rendered a splendid promenade, most brilliantly lighted with glass chandeliers and lustres. This blaze of light is further increased by reflection from the large glasses and mirrors which are found in every room. In England, the glasses are pitiful to a degree. In France, even in the inns, they reach in one undivided plate from the top of the room to the bottom. The French furniture moreover is infinitely more magnificent than in England. Curtains, chair-covers, &c. are all of silk, and the chairs fashioned according to the designs of artists. The French music too, such as attends on their parties, exceeds that of England; in a few words, a party in France is a spectacle; it is arranged with art; and where there is much art, there will always be some taste.

In the neighbourhood of Lyons are numerous chateaus, most delightfully situated, with lawns, pleasure-grounds, gardens, and green-houses, in the English taste. In the summer season, public breakfasts are almost daily given by one or other of the possessors. Marquees are then erected on the lawn, and all the military bands in the town attend. The day is consumed in dancing, which is often protracted so late in the night, as almost to trespass on the day following. These kind of parties are perhaps too favourable for intrigue, to suit English or American manners, but they are certainly delightful in a degree, and recall to one's fancy the images of poetry.

The French ladies, as I believe I have before mentioned, are fond of habiting themselves as harvesters: they frequently visit the farmers thus*incog.* and hire themselves for the day. Though the farmer knows them, it is the established custom that he should favour the sport by pretending ignorance, and treating them in every respect as if they were what they seemed. This is another means of indulging that general disposition to gallantry which characterizes a Frenchwoman. They must have lovers of all degrees and qualities; for vanity is at the bottom of this assumed humility.

Lodging at Lyons, in which I include board, is extremely cheap: for about thirty pounds per annum you may board in the first houses, and I was informed that every one is welcome but Italians. The French have an extreme contempt for Italians. A house at Lyons may likewise be hired very cheap. The pleasantest houses, however, are situated out of the town; and I have no doubt, but that such an house as would cost in England one hundred per annum, might be hired in the environs of Lyons, in the loveliest country in the world, by the sides of the Rhone and the Saone, and with a view of the Alps, for about twenty-five Louis annual rent. Every house has a garden, and many of them mulberry orchards, a wood, and pleasure-grounds.

We left Lyons on the morning of the third day after our arrival, much pleased with our stay, and with the general appearance of the city and the inhabitants. Avignon was the next main point of our destination. As the distance between Lyons and Avignon is about 120 miles, we distributed our journey into three divisions, and as many days.

Lyons is connected by a stone bridge with the beautiful village La Guillotiere; it consists of twenty arches, and is upwards of 1200 feet in length. I believe I have before observed, that the provincial bridges, as well as the roads in France, are infinitely superior to any thing of the kind in England, and that the cause of this superiority is, that they are under the controul and supervision of the government. Every thing connected with the facility of general access is considered as of public concern, and therefore as an object of government. In England, the roads are made and mended by the vicinity. In France, this business belongs to the state and to the administration of the province.

For many miles from Lyons, the road continued very various, occasionally hill and dale, bordered by hedges, in which were flowers and flowering shrubs, that perfumed the air very delightfully. It is not uncommon to find even orange trees in the open fields: the very air of the country seemed different from any through which I had before passed. There were many of the fields planted with mulberry trees; I observed that this tree seemed to flourish best where nothing else would grow—on stony and gravelly soils. This indeed seems to be the common excellence of the mulberry and the vine, that they may be both cultivated on lands which would otherwise be barren.

We passed several flower-mills on the river Gere; a beautiful stream, occasionally very thickly wooded, and passing in a channel, which, as seen from the road, has any appearance but that of a level. The smaller rivers in France, like the bye lanes, are infinitely more beautiful than the larger; the water, passing over a bed of gravel, is limpid and transparent to a degree, and the grounds through which they roll, being left in their natural rudeness, have a character of wildness, romance, and picturesque, which is not to be found in the greater

71

navigable streams. An evening stroll along their banks, would favour the imagination of a poet. I feel some surprize, that a greater proportion of the writers of France are not their descriptive poets.

The Gere is animated by numerous flower-mills; there are likewise many paper-mills. They chiefly pleased me by their lovely situation. Mademoiselle St. Sillery repeatedly sung a line of a French song, "O that I were a miller's maid." It is but justice to this lady to say, that she possessed a sensibility to the charms of Nature, which is seldom found in tempers so apparently thoughtless.

As we passed several cottages by the road-side, we saw the peasant girls spinning; some of them were working in silk, others in cotton. They all seemed happy, gay, and noisy; and where there were one or two of them together, seemed to interrupt their labour by playing with each other. It is impossible that a people of this kind can feel their labour. Some of them, moreover, were really handsome.

We reached Vienne to a late dinner, and resolved to remain there for the night. Our inn had nothing to recommend it but its situation. Our dinner however was plentiful, and what is not very common, was very well dressed. The vegetables would not have disgraced an hotel in London. Potatoes are becoming as common in France as in England, and the greens of all sorts are to the full as good. "Confess," said Mr. Younge, "that you would not have dined better in London, and the price will be about one-fourth." "And confess," said Mademoiselle St. Sillery, "that in London you would not have had such an accompaniment to your dinner, such a lovely sky, and a garden so luxuriant in flowers." The windows were open, and looked backwards into the garden, which was certainly beautiful and luxuriant to a degree. On the other side of the hedge, which was at the further extremity, some one was playing on the flageolet: the tune was simple and sweet, and perfectly in unison with the scene. "Who is it," demanded I, "that plays so well?" "Some one who has been at the wars," said Madame Younge. "The French boys in the army, if they signalize themselves by any act of bravery, have sometimes one year's leave of absence given them as a reward. This is some fifer who has obtained this leave."

We had coffee, as is still the custom in the provinces, immediately after dinner; it was brought in by a sweet girl, who blushed and smiled most charmingly as she fell over the corner of a chair. Her father afterwards related her simple history in brief. She was the belle in Vienne, and was courted by two or three of her own condition, but was inflexibly attached to a young conscript. "You will doubtless hear him before you depart," continued the landlord, "for he is almost always behind that garden hedge, playing on his flageolet."—The lover it seems was the young fifer. Mademoiselle St. Sillery now became very restless. "You wish to see this gentleman," said Mrs. Younge to her, smiling. Mademoiselle made no other answer than by beckoning to me, and in the same moment putting on her bonnet. I could do no less than accompany her. We went into the garden, and thence over a rough stile into the fields. Much to our disappointment, Corydon was not to be seen. "I am sure he must be a gentleman, by his taste and delicacy," said Mademoiselle.

We had not time to see much of the town, nor did it appear much to deserve it. It is certainly very prettily situated on the Gere and the Rhone, and is surrounded by hills, which give it pleasantness and effect. It seemed to us to be comparatively a busy and thriving town—I say comparatively, for as compared with the towns of England or America, its trade was contemptible. There are two or three hardware manufactories, where the steel is said to be well tempered. The town is of great antiquity, and carries its age in its face. The streets are irregular; the houses dark; one room in almost every house is very large, and all the others most inconveniently small. This is the invariable characteristic of the house architecture of towns of a certain age.

I understood from inquiry, that, with the exception of wood for fuel, every thing was very reasonable in Vienne. Provisions were in great plenty, and very cheap. The town, as I have said, is dull, but the environs, the fields, and the gardens, delightful.

On the following day we continued our journey, and having sent our horses forward, took our seats in the carriage with the ladies. The young conscript seemed to fill the head of Mademoiselle St. Sillery. "These kind of adventures," said she, "are not so romantic in France as they would be in England, and more particularly since the conscription makes no distinction of ranks. It is reckoned an honour, or at least no disgrace, to be a private in the conscripts. It is incredible, how great a number of gentlemen fill the ranks of the French army. A foreigner cannot conceive it."

Mr. Younge confirmed this remark, and imputed much of the success of the French arms to the spirit of honour and emulation which resulted from this constitution. "Every conscript," said he, "indeed every French soldier, knows that all the dignities of the army are open to him, and he may one day be himself a General, if he can render himself prominent. The chevaliers, moreover, are not only animated by a gallant spirit themselves, but they infuse it into the army, and give it a character and self-esteem, the effect of which is truly wonderful."

We passed through some pleasant villages, and amongst these Condrieux, which is celebrated in France for its excellent wine: it is thick and sweet, and resembles Tent. The price is high, and as usual in the wine countries, none that is good is to be had on the spot. The country about this village was rugged, uneven, but wild and picturesque; it resembled no part that I had before seen. The fields were still planted with mulberry trees, and the hedges (for the country is thickly enclosed), were perfumed with scented shrubs. We saw some women driving oxen carts. One of them was a tall, and as far as good features went, a good-looking girl, but her fate sun-burnt, and her legs naked. She handled the whip moreover with great strength, and apparently with little temper. She returned our smile as we passed her, but bowed her body to the ladies. "Is it possible," said I, "that there can be any gentleness in that creature?" "If by gentleness you mean a taste for gallantry, and an expectation of it as her right," replied Mr. Younge, "she has it as much as any Parisian belle. In France, indeed, gallantry is like water; it is considered as a thing of common right; it is as unnatural to withhold it as it is natural to receive it. If you were to meet that lady in a village walk, she would think herself very ill treated, if you had not a compliment on your tongue, and at least the appearance of a sentiment in your heart."

Several waggons of the country passed us; their construction was awkward to a degree. The French are very far behind the English in the ingenuity of the lower order of their artisans. A French watchmaker usually exceeds an English one; but a French blacksmith, a French carpenter, are as infinitely inferior. The things in common use are execrable: not a window that shuts close, not a door that fits; every thing clumsy, rough hewn, and as if made by Robinson Crusoe and his man Friday.

We reached St. Valier to sleep. It is a small town, but prettily situated, and the environs fertile, highly cultivated, and naturally beautiful. The landlord of the inn was a true Boniface; he had nothing of the Frenchman but his civility to the ladies. In assisting Mrs. Younge from the carriage, he contrived it so awkwardly that he fell on his back, and pulled the lady upon him; the matter, however, was a mere trifle to a Frenchwoman, and had no other effect but to raise her colour. If there are any ladies in a carriage, it is the invariable privilege of the French hosts that they hand them from their seats. Boniface, however, compensated his personal awkwardness by setting before us an excellent supper; indeed, the farther we travelled, the cheaper and the better became our fare. The hostess was likewise a true character: she made some observations so free, and even indelicate, in the hearing of the ladies, as in some degree confounded me. But modesty is certainly no part of the virtues of a Frenchwoman.

My bed-chamber was scented with orange trees which occupied one end of the room. The hostess herself came up to wish me good night, and to express her compassion for Mademoiselle St. Sillery and me, because truly, not being married together, we were obliged to sleep separate, though so near each other. It came very strongly into my mind, that she had been making a similar observation to Mademoiselle. The French women certainly talk with a freedom which would startle an English or American female. With the greatest possible *sang froid* they will seat themselves on the side of the bed, and remain in conversation with you till they have fairly seen you in. They seem indeed to consider this office as a matter of course. They enter your chamber at all times with equal freedom; and if there happen to be two or more filles-de-chambre, they will very coolly seat themselves and converse together. There is indeed but one invariable rule in France, and that is, that a fille-de-chambre is company for an emperor.

Being very tired, I had slept sounder than usual, when I was called by the landlady, accompanied by Mademoiselle St. Sillery. The latter indeed remained at the door of the apartment, but the good-humoured boisterous landlady awoke me with some violence by a toss of the clothes. "Rise, Monsieur," said she, "and attend your mistress through the town; she wants a walk. Shame upon a chevalier to sleep, whilst so much beauty is awake!" I have translated literally, that I may give an idea of that tone of compliment, and even of language, which characterizes the French men and women, in speaking to or of each other. Mademoiselle St. Sillery, in the course of our journey, was as warmly complimented for her beauty by the women as by the gentlemen. One woman in particular, and an elderly one, embraced her with a kind of rapture, saying at the same time, that she was as lovely as an angel. This extravagance of the women towards each other is peculiar to France, or at least I have never seen it elsewhere.

As the morning was delightful, we resolved, much to the discontent of the landlady, to reach Thein to breakfast. The horses were accordingly ordered, and after much reluctance, and some grumbling, we procured them, and departed.

The road was continually on the ascent, and in every mile opened the most lovely prospects. The trees in this part of France are uncommonly beautiful; and where there are any meadows, as along the banks of the rivers, they are adorned with the sweetest flowers, which here grow wild, and attain a more than garden-sweetness and brilliancy. The birds, moreover, were singing merrily, and all Nature seemed animate and gay. I felt truly happy, and Mademoiselle St. Sillery was in such life and spirits, that it was not without difficulty that we detained her in her seat.

Thein, where we breakfasted, was the Teyna of the Romans: it is delightfully situated at the bottom of an hill, called the Hermitage, and celebrated over all Europe and the world for its rich wines. The soil on which these vineyards grow is a very light loam, supported by a pan of granite, in which it resembles what is denominated in England the Norfolk soil. Another hill on the opposite side of the river produces the wine called the *côte rotie*. The average yearly produce is nearly one thousand hogsheads, and the price of the wine on the spot, in retail, is about 3s. 6d. English money the bottle. From the window of the apartment in which we breakfasted, we had a view of the town of Tournon, and the ruins of an old castle, which very pleasantly invited our imagination into former times.

Proceeding on our journey, ourselves, our horses, and our carriage, were all transported over the river in a boat, which instead of being ferried over by men, was dragged over by a pulley and rope on the opposite side. I should imagine that this method is not very safe, but it certainly saves labour and trouble; and it is impossible to build a bridge over a river like the Rhone and the Isere. This river is very rapid, but not very clear. Its banks are rocky, hilly, and occasionally open into the most beautiful scenery which it is possible for poet or painter to conceive. The Isere was well known to the ancients.

We dined at Valence, which is delightfully situated in a plain six or eight miles in breadth. It was well known to the Romans by the name of Valentia, and is supposed to have been so called from its healthy scite, or, according to other writers, from the military strength of its situation. The rocks in its vicinity gave it an air of great wildness, and there are many popular stories as to its former inhabitants. The town however has nothing but its scite to recommend it. The streets are narrow, without air, and therefore very dirty. There is a church of the most remote antiquity: I had not leisure to examine it, but its external appearance corresponded with its reputed age. It was evidently built by the Romans, but has been so much altered, that it is difficult to say whether its original destination was a theatre or a temple. In the Roman ages, theatres were national works, and therefore corresponded with the characteristic greatness of the empire, and every thing which belonged to it. What play-house in Europe would survive two thousand years! This single reflection appears to me to put the comparative greatness of the Romans in a most striking point of view. They built, indeed, for posterity, and their architecture had the character of their writing—it passed unhurt down the stream of time.

The inn-keeper at Valence amused us much by his empty pomposity. He was a complete character, but civility made no part of his qualities. His dinner however was excellent and possible humour on the following day. Mrs. Younge replied very smartly to some questions of her husband. This lady had a true affection, and I will take upon me to say, that the fidelity of Mr. Younge was such as to merit it.

Our road to Montelimart, our first or second stage (I really forget which) was lined on each side with chesnut and mulberry trees. We passed many vineyards, and innumerable orchards. For mile succeeding to mile it was more like a garden than an open country. The fields, wherever there was the least moisture, were covered with flowers; the hedges of the vineyards breathed forth a most delightful odour; there was every thing to cheer the heart and to refresh the senses. Some of the cottages which we passed were delightfully situated: they invariably, however, whether good or bad, were without glass to their windows; and the climate is so dry and so mild, that they sleep with them thus exposed.

Montelimart is situated in a plain, which is covered with corn and vineyards; and being here and there studded with tufts of chesnut trees, has a rural and pleasing appearance. It is built on the bank of a small river which runs from the Rhone, is a walled town, and has usually a tolerably strong garrison. It has the same character, however, as all the other towns on the Rhone—the streets are narrow, and the houses low. In plain words, the town is execrable, but its scite delightful.

From Montelimart to where we slept, the name of which I have not noted, the country improved in beauty; but we passed many peasant women, who certainly were not so beautiful as the country. Their costume reminded me very forcibly of Dutch toys—very broad-brimmed straw hats, and petticoats not reaching to the knees. Add to this, naked legs, &c. Our ladies smiled at my astonishment, and I smiled too, when I reflected to what feelings and to what ideas people might be reduced by habit. In the West Indies, a white lady feels no reluctance, no modest confusion, at the sight of the nakedness of her male slave; and Madame Younge and Mademoiselle St. Sillery, certainly the most modest women in France, only smiled at my surprise, when these short petticoated women passed me. So it is with custom. Time was, that many things startled me, which I can now see or hear without wonder. But nothing, I hope, will ever eradicate that modesty which is inseparable from a reflecting mind, and which acts as a barrier against inordinate passions.

The peasantry in this part of the country seemed very poor, though contented and happy. Many of them were employed on a labour for which their pay must have been very small—picking stones from the fields, and dung from the roads. The dung is dried and burned, and is said to be an healthy fuel to those who use it.

On the following day we dined at Orange, but did not remain long enough to examine the town, which was well worthy of minute attention. Mademoiselle St. Sillery was seized with the symptoms of an indisposition, which happily passed away, but whilst it lasted, left us no inclination for any other employment but to assist and console her, and to press forwards to Avignon, to procure medical assistance. Fortunately, it turned out to be nothing but a mere dizziness resulting from exposure to the sun.

Under these circumstances we reached Avignon on the evening of the fourth day after leaving Lyons; and whether the fear of the physician had any effect, so much is certain, that Mademoiselle seemed to have completed her recovery almost in the same instant in which the battlements of the city saluted her eyes.

## CHAP. XIX.

*Avignon—Situation—Climate—Streets and Houses—Public*
*Buildings—Palace—Cathedral—Petrarch and Laura—Society*
*at Avignon—Ladies—Public Walks—Prices of*
*Provisions—Markets.*

WHEN we left Angers, we had ordered our letters to be addressed for us at Avignon. I was daily in expectation of receiving one of a very important nature, and General Armstrong, who was in the habit of a state correspondence with Marseilles, and was allowed for that purpose an extra post, had promised to dispatch it for me to Avignon, as soon as it should reach him. This circumstance delayed us for some days at Avignon; but I believe none of us regretted a delay, which gave us time to see and to survey this celebrated city and its neighbourhood.

The situation of this city is in a plain, equally fertile and beautiful, about fifteen miles in breadth and ten in length. On the south and east it is circled by a chain of mountains. The plain is divided into cultivated fields, in which are grown wheat, barley, saffron, silk, and madder. The cultivation is so clean and exact, as to give the grounds the appearance of a garden. As the French farms are usually on a small scale, they are invariably kept cleaner than those in England and America. Not a weed is suffered to remain on the ground. The French want nothing but a more enlarged knowledge and a greater capital, to rival the English husbandmen. They have the same industry, and take perhaps more pride in the appearance of their fields. This detailed attention greatly improves the face of the country; for miles succeeding miles it has the air of a series of parks and gardens. The English mansion is alone wanting to complete the beauty of the scenery. From the high ground in the city nothing can be finer than the prospect over the plain and surrounding country. The Rhone is there seen rolling its animated through meadows covered with olive trees, and at the foot of hills invested with vineyards. The ruined arches of the old bridge carry the imagination back into the ancient history of the town. On the opposite side of the Rhone are the sunny plains of Laguedoc, which, when refreshed by the wind, breathe odours and perfumes from a thousand wild herbs and flowers. Mont Ventoux, in the province of Dauphiny, closes the prospect to the North: its high summit covered with snow, whilst its sides are robed in all the charms of vegetable nature. On the east are the abrupt rocks and precipices of Vaucluse, distant about five leagues, and which complete, as it were, the garden wall around Avignon and its territory.

The climate of Avignon, though so strangely inveighed against by Petrarch, is at once healthy and salubrious. There are certainly very rapid transitions from extreme heat to extreme cold, but from this very circumstance neither the intensity of the heat nor of the cold, is of sufficient duration to be injurious to health or pleasure. The air, except in actual rain, is always dry, and the sky is an etherial Italian blue, scarcely ever obscured by a cloud. When the rains come on they are very violent, but fall at once. The sun then bursts out, and the face of Nature appears more gay, animated and splendid than before. I do not remember, that amongst all the pictures of the great masters, I have ever seen a landscape in which a southern country was represented after one of these showers. Homer has described it with equal force and beauty, in one of his similies: but as the book is not before me, I must refer to the memory of the classic reader.

There is one heavy detraction, however, from the excellence of the Avignonese climate. This is the wind denominated the Vent de Bize. The peculiar situation of Avignon, at the mouth of a long avenue of mountains, gives rise to this wind: it collects in the narrow channel of the mountains, and bursts, as from the mouth of a barrel, on the town and plain. Its violence certainly exceeds what is common in European climates, but it is considered as healthy, and it very rarely does any considerable damage. Augustus Cæsar was so persuaded of its salutary character, that he deified it, as it were, by raising an altar to it under the name of the Circian wind. The winters of Avignon, however, are sometimes rendered by it most distressingly cold. The Rhone is frequently covered with ice sufficiently strong to support loaded carts, and the olive trees sometimes perish to their roots.

Avignon is surrounded by walls built by successive Popes; they still remain in perfect beauty and preservation, and much augment, particularly in a distant view, the beauty of the town. They are composed of free-stone, are flanked at regular distances with square towers, and surmounted with battlements. The public walks are round the foot of this wall. The alleys fronting the river, and which are bordered by noble elms, are the summer promenade—here all the fashion of the city assemble in the evening, and walk, and sport, and romp on the banks. In the winter, the public walk is on the opposite side. The fields likewise have their share, and the environs being naturally beautiful, the spectacle on a summer's evening is gay and delightful in the extreme.

The interior of the city is ill built: the streets are narrow and irregular, and the pavement is most troublesomely rough. There is not a lamp, except at the houses of the better kind of people; the funds of the town are still good, but they are all expended on the roads, public walks, and dinners. The necessity of a constant attention to paving and lighting, never enters into the heads of a French town-administration; they seem to think that the whole business is done when the town is once paved. From the nature of the climate, however, the streets are necessarily clean. A hot drying sun, and frequent driving winds, remove or consume all the ordinary rubbish; or if anything be left, the winter torrent of the Rhone, rising above its bed, sweeps it all before it. Avignon, therefore, is naturally a clean city. The police, moreover, is very commendably attentive, to the price of provisions, and to the cleanliness of the markets.

I had the curiosity to enter some of the houses, and found them to correspond with what I have before described as constituting the character of house-architecture in the thirteenth and fourteenth centuries. They had one large room, and all the others small; a great waste of timber and work in their construction; the walls being built as thick as if intended for fortifications, and the beams being large timber trees. Our ancestors thought they could never build too substantially.

The palace, the former residence of the Papal Legates, is well worthy of being visited: it was founded by Benedict the Twelfth but is better known as the subject of the elegant invective of Petrarch. The arsenal still remains, containing 4000 stand of arms and as these instruments of war are ranged according to their respective æras, the spectacle is interesting, and to antiquaries may be instructive. The papal chair, from respect to its antiquity, still remains, but the pannels of the state rooms, which were composed of polished cedar, have disappeared. The most curious parts of the palace, however, are the subterraneous passages, the entrance to which is usually through some part of the pillars; perfectly imperceptible till pointed out by the guide. According to the tradition of the town, these passages have been the scene of many a deed of darkness. A statue of Hercules was found on the scite of the palace, and buried by Pope Urban, that the figure of a Heathen Deity might not disgrace a papal town.

The cathedral still retains many of its ancient decorations, and amongst these, the monument of Pope John, who died in the year 1384. In the year 1759, the body was taken up to be removed, when it was found entire, and with some of the vestments retaining their original colour. The first wrapper round the body was a robe of purple silk, which was then enveloped in black velvet embroidered in gold and pearls; the hands had white satin gloves, and were crossed over the breast. The above description is exhibited in writing to all travellers. The monument of Benedict the Twelfth is likewise here. This Pope was as remarkable for his integrity of life and simplicity of manners, as for his humility. There are many illustrious men who lie buried beneath the cathedral, but as I could give little account of them but their names, I shall pass them over.

We next visited the convent of St. Claire, where Petrarch first beheld his mistress. From respect to the poet, or to his mistress, this convent has survived the fury of the times, and is still entire. The description of the first meeting of Laura and Petrarch is perhaps the best, because the most simple and unlaboured part of his works.—"It was on one of the lovely mornings of the spring of the year, the morning of April 6th, 1327, that being at matins in the convent of St. Claire, I first beheld my Laura. Her robe was green embroidered with violets. Her features, her air, her deportment, announced something which did not belong to mortal. Her figure was graceful beyond the imagination of a poet—her eyes beamed with tenderness, and her eye-brows were black as ebony. Her golden ringlets, interwoven by the fingers of Love, played upon shoulders whiter than snow. Her neck, in its harmony and proportion, was a model for painters; and her complexion breathed that life and soul which no painters can give When she opened her mouth, you saw the beauty of pearls, and the sweetness of the morning rose. The mildness of her look, the modesty of her gait, the soft harmony of her voice, must be seen and felt to be conceived. Gaiety and gentleness breathed around her, and these so pure and happily attempered, as to render love a virtue, and admiration a kind of divine tribute."

Our curiosity naturally passed from the convent of St. Claire to the church of the Cordeliers, where Laura is reputed to have reposed in peace. Her tomb is in a small chapel, dark, damp, and even noisome: it is indicated only by a flat unadorned stone. The inscription, which is in Gothic letters, is rendered illegible by time. The congenial nature of Francis the First of France caused the tomb to be opened, and a leaden box was found, containing some bones, and a copy of verses, the subject of which was the attachment of the two lovers. Petrarch, with all his conceits, which are sometimes as cold as the snows on Mount Ventoux, well merits his reputation. His verses are polished, and his thoughts almost always elegant and poetical. He must not be judged, on the point of a correct taste, with those who followed him. He was the first, as it were, in the field; he is to be considered as an original poet in a dark age; or, according to his own beautiful comparison, as a nightingale singing through the thick foliage of the beech tree. Petrarch was truly an original; I know no one to whom he can be compared. He has no resemblance to any English, French, or Italian. He has more ease, more elegance, and a more poetic vein than Prior; he resembles Cowley in his conceits, and Waller in his grace and sweetness. He possesses, moreover, one quality in common with the Classic poets of Italy—that he never has, and perhaps never will be, sufficiently translated. No translation can give the elegant neatness of his language. He is simple, tender, and sweet as his own Laura: time has stampt his reputation, and posterity will receive him to her last limit.

We next visited the convent of the Celestins, which was founded by Charles the Sixth of France, and in its architecture and dimensions is worthy of a royal founder. The piety of the early ages has done more to ornament the kingdoms of Europe than either public or private magnificence. If we would become properly sensible how much we owe to the early ages, let us divest a kingdom of what has been built by our ancestors; let us pull down the churches, the convents, and the temples, and what shall we leave?—The present town-administration of Avignon extends a very commendable attention to its several public buildings, the consequence of which is, that the town flourishes, and is much visited both by travellers and distant residents.

Avignon, however, is chiefly celebrated for its hospitals, the liberal foundation and endowment of which have originated, perhaps in the misfortunes of the city, and in the sympathy which is usually felt for evils which we ourselves have experienced. Avignon has suffered as much as Florence itself by the plague. In the year 1334 the city was almost depopulated by this dreadful pestilence. It was in the nature of a dry leprosy; the skin peeled off in white scales, and the body wasted till the disease reached the vitals. In fourteen years afterwards the city was again attacked, and the beautiful Laura became its victim. It is stated to have swept off upwards of one hundred thousand inhabitants. The reigning pope contrived to escape the contagion by shutting himself up in his palace, carefully excluding the air, and heating the rooms. Another period of fourteen years elapsed, and the plague again made its appearance, and nearly twenty thousand people, including a dozen cardinals and an hundred bishops, fell its victims. Of late years, there has fortunately been no appearance of this horrible disease. It was at the time imputed to an extraordinary drought, attended by an uncommon heat and stillness of the air, which, being without motion, and confined as it were in a narrow channel, became putrid and pestilential. The vent de bize is perhaps a greater blessing to this country than it has been imagined.

Avignon, with the above exceptions, would be a delightful place of residence to a foreigner, and particularly if his circumstances permitted him to live in an extended society. It constitutes, as it were, a little kingdom in itself, and the inhabitants have clearly and distinctly a character, and peculiar manners belonging to themselves.

We visited the public walks of the town every evening during our stay, and as the weather was delightful, and there was a division of soldiers with their bands of music on the spot, they were always thronged, and always gay and animated to a degree.

The Avignonese ladies appeared to me very beautiful, and whether it was fancy or reality, I thought I could trace in many of them the features which Petrarch has assigned to Laura. I no doubt whatever, but that the recorded loves of these accomplished persons have a very strong influence on the character of the town. If I should have an Avignonese for a mistress, I should most certainly expect to find in her some of the characteristic traits of Laura. It must not, indeed, be concealed, that these ladies have not the reputation of being virtuous in the extreme: to say the truth, they are considered as dissolute, and as having little restraint even in their married conduct. I cannot say this of them from any thing which I observed myself—to me they appeared gay, tender and interesting.

In speaking of ladies, it would be unpardonable to omit something of their dress. The ladies of Avignon follow the Paris fashions, but have too much natural elegance to adopt them in extremes. On the evening parade, they were habited in silk robes, which in their form resembled collegiate gowns, and being of the gayest colours, gave the public walk a resemblance to a flower-garden. Lace caps were the only covering of their heads. The necks were not so exposed as at Paris, but were open as is usual in. England and America in full dress. The gown was likewise silk, embroidered in silver, gold, or worked flowers. The shoes of velvet, with silver or gold clasps. The terms were naked almost up to the shoulders, indeed almost indecently so. Being strangers, we were of course objects of curiosity; when our eyes, however, met those of the gazers, they invariably saluted us with a friendly smile. Mademoiselle St. Sillery was much distressed that she had no dress so tasty as those of the ladies. We could not at last persuade her to accompany us. This young lady, with all her charms, and she possessed as many as ever fell to the lot of woman, had certainly her share of vanity—an assertion, however, which I should not have the presumption to make, if she had not herself most frequently acknowledged it.

Every thing connected with household economy is extremely cheap at Avignon; a circumstance which must be imputed as much to the moderation of the inhabitants as to the plenty of the country. An Avignonese family seems to have no idea of a dinner in common with an Englishman or an American. A couple of over-roasted fowls will be meat enough for a party of a dozen. The most common dish is, I believe, a fowl stewed down into soup, with rice, highly seasoned. It is certainly very savoury, only that according to French cookery, too much is made of the fowl.

The Avignonese, whilst under the papal jurisdiction, bore a general reputation for the utmost profligacy both of principles and conduct. This character has now passed away, and, with the exception of what is termed gallantry, the Avignonese seem a gay, moral, and harmless people. The poetry of Petrarch is perhaps too much read, and it is impossible to read him without inspiring a warmth of feeling and imagination, which is not very friendly to a correct virtue. Plato would certainly have banished him from his republic, and the Avignonese would do well to keep him out of their schools and houses. They will catch his ardour, who want his moral sense and religious principles.

We took our leave of Avignon, much delighted with the town and its inhabitants, and, as I have before said, I saw many figures which recalled most forcibly to my imagination the Laura of Petrarch. It may be perhaps said, that every one has an image of his own fancy, which he assigns to Laura, and that from the general description of the poet, it is impossible to collect any thing of the personal lineaments of his mistress. This is very true; but it is equally so, that the ladies of Avignon appear to have certain characteristic features, and that many of them possess that soft, sweet, and supreme beauty, which inspired Petrarch to sing in strains, which still sound melodious in the ears of his posterity.

Avignon is the capital of the department of Vaucluse, the department being so named rather from the celebrity of the poet, than from its local relations.

### CHAP. XX.

*Departure from Avignon—Olive and Mulberry Fields—Orgon—St. Canat—French Divorces—Inn at St. Canat—Air—Situation—Cathedral—Society—Provisions—Price of Land—Marseilles—Conclusion.*

THE letters which I had expected reached me at Avignon, and the result of their perusal was the information, that my presence was necessary in America. I have not, however, contracted so much of the impertinence of a Frenchman by my tour in France, as to trouble the reader of my Notes with my domestic affairs. Suffice it therefore to say, that some family occurrences, of which I obtained some previous information, required my immediate departure from France, and that in consequence I resolved to embark at Marseilles.

With this resolution, therefore, I left Avignon for Marseilles, a distance of about seventy miles. We divided it therefore into two days; arranging so as to reach St. Canat on the first night, and Marseilles on the second.

The road to Orgon, where we dined, presented us with a great variety of scenery, though the surface was rather level. All the country was covered with olive and mulberry trees, and innumerable fruit-trees grew up wild in the fields, as likewise flowering shrubs in the hedges. The climate of this part of France is so delightful, that every thing here grows spontaneously which is raised only by the most laborious exertions in northern countries. The cottages which we passed on the road were picturesque to a degree: they were usually thatched, and vines or barberry trees, or honey-suckles, entirely enveloped the walls or casements. The peasantry, moreover, though without stockings, appeared happy; the women were singing, and the men, in the intervals of their work, playing with true French frivolity. We saw many women working in the fields: the French women are invariably industrious and active. It may be supposed that this labour and exposure to a southern sun is not very favourable to beauty. Accordingly, we saw few good-looking damsels, but many with good shapes and good eyes. How is it, that the French, so generally gallant, can suffer their women to take the fork and hoe, and work so laboriously in the fields?

Orgon had nothing which merits even mention; I believe, however, it was well known to the ancients, and is mentioned in some of the Latin itineraries. A convent, very picturesquely situated, is now converted into a manufacturing establishment. The town is surrounded by chalk-hills and quarries, from which is dug a free-stone, of the most delicate white. The town, on the whole, had an air of rusticity and recluseness which might have delighted a romantic imagination.

Between Orgon and St. Canat we travelled in a road occasionally bordered by almond trees. The country on each side was rather barren, but being an intermixture of rock and plain and being moreover new to us, it did not appear tedious or uninteresting. We passed several houses of the better sort, some in ruins, others evidently inhabited by a class of people for whom they were not intended. This is one of the effects of the Revolution. Where the proprietor emigrated, or was assassinated, the nearest tenant moved into the mansion-house, and if he distinguished himself by a violent and patriotic jacobinism, his possession, for a mere trifle to the national fund, was converted into a right. In this manner innumerable low ruffians have obtained the estates and houses of their lords; but, faithful to their old habits and early origin, they abuse only what they possess; live in the stables, and convert the castle into a barn, a granary, a brew-house, a manufactory, or sometimes dilapidate it brick by brick, as their convenience may require.

The inn at St. Canat will be long remembered by me, for the unusual circumstance of a most hearty welcome from a good-humoured host, a widower, and his two daughters. The eldest was the most beautiful brunette I have ever seen. She was as coquettish as if educated in Paris, and as easy, as familiar, as inclined to gallantry, as this description of ladies, in France at least, universally are. She had been married during the æra of jacobinism, and had divorced her husband, *because they could not agree.* "He was so triste, and withal very jealous, which was the more absurd, because he was old."—This young woman was tall, elegant, and with the most fascinating features; her age might be about four and twenty; her teeth were the whitest in the world, and her smile was a paradise of sweets. She had the fault, however, of all the French filles—a most invincible loquacity, and would not move from the chamber till repeatedly admonished to call me early in the morning.

I was awoke in the morning by a sweet-toned lark, which rising in the ethereal vault of Heaven, made his watch-tower, as the poet calls it, ring with his matin song. I know nothing more pleasing to a traveller than to pass a night at one of these provincial inns, provided he gets a good bed and clean blankets. The moon shines through his casement with a soft and clear splendor unparalleled in humid climates; and in the morning he is awoke by the singing of birds, whilst his senses are hailed by the perfume of flowers and by the freshness of a pure æther.

Having resumed our journey, we reached Aix at an early hour on the following day, and passed an hour very pleasantly in walking over the town and neighbourhood.

Aix, the capital of Provence, is very pleasantly situated in a valley, surrounded by hills, which give it an air of recluseness, and romantic retirement, without being so close as to prevent the due circulation of air. It is surrounded by a wall, but which, from long neglect, originating perhaps in its inutility, has become dilapidated, and interests only as an ancient ruin. In the former ages, when France was subdivided into dutchies and minor kingdoms, and when her neighbours were more powerful, such walls were a necessary defence to the town: a change in manners and government has now rendered them useless, and in few centuries they will wholly disappear all over Europe. The interior of the town very well corresponds with the importance of its first aspect. It is well paved, the houses are all fronted with white stone, and the air being clear, it always looks clean and sprightly. Many of them, moreover, have balconies, and some of them are upon a scale, both outside and inside, which is not excelled by Bath in England. Aix is almost the only town next to Tours, in which an English gentleman could fix a comfortable residence. The society is good, and to a stranger of genteel appearance, perfectly accessible either with or without introduction.

The cathedral of Aix is an immense edifice; the architecture is the oldest Gothic, and has all the strength, the substance, and I was going to add, all the tastelessness which characterizes that Order. The front is ornamented with figures of saints, prophets, and angels, grouped together in a manner the most absurd, and executed as if by the hands of a working bricklayer. The grand portal, however is very striking. On the side of the great altar is the magnificent tomb of the Counts of Provence; the figures here, however, are as ridiculous as the style itself is grand. The Gothic architects had better ideas of proportion than of delicacy or beauty; they seldom err on the former point, whilst their execution in the latter is contemptible in the extreme. Our Saviour, and the Virgin Mary, have always enough to do on every tomb in France; they are invariably introduced together, sometimes in a manner and with circumstances, which really shock any one of common piety. Several pictures, and some ancient jewellery, which have survived the Revolution, are still shewn to all strangers: amongst them is a golden rose, which Pope Innocent the Fourth gave to one of the Counts of Provence six hundred years since.

There are two or three other churches and convents, but which have suffered so much by the execrable Revolution, as to have little left that is worthy of remark. The piety of the inhabitants of Aix, however, saved the greater part of the pictures and jewellery; and with still more piety, have returned them to the churches.

The promenade, or public walk, equals, if not excells, any thing of the kind in Europe—it consists of three alleys, shaded by four rows of most noble elms, in the middle of a wide street, the houses on each side being on the most magnificent scale, and inhabited by the first people of the city and province. There were several parties walking there even at the early hour in the morning when we saw it, and I understood upon enquiry, that in the evening it is exceedingly thronged both with walkers and carriages.

I did not omit to make my usual enquiries, as to the prices of land, provisions, and the state of society, for a foreigner who should select it as a place of residence. The following was the result: Land within a few miles of Aix, is very reasonable; in a large purchase it will not exceed five or six pounds (English money) per acre. In rating French and English purchases, there is one considerable point of difference: English estates are usually mentioned as being worth so many years purchase, in which the purchase is rated according to the rent, and the rent is considered as being the annual value of the land. In France, where there is scarcely such a thing as an annual pecuniary rent equal to the annual value of the land, the price must be estimated by the acre. In large purchases, therefore, as I have said before, land is very cheap: in small purchases it is very dear. The difference indeed is surprising, but must be imputed to the strong repugnance of the small proprietors to part with their paternal lands.

In the town there are some very handsome houses: a palace almost, with a garden of some acres, an orchard, and land enough for four horses and three cows, may be hired for about thirty pounds per annum.

Provisions of all kinds are in the greatest possible plenty: fish is to be had in great abundance, and the best quality; meat is likewise very reasonable, and tolerably good; bread is about a penny English by the pound; and vegetables, as in other provincial towns, so cheap as scarcely to be worth selling.

The baths of Aix are very celebrated, and the town is much visited by valetudinarians: they are chiefly recommended in scorbutic humours, colds, rheumatisms, palsies, and consumptions. The waters are warm, and have in fact no taste but that of warm water.

Upon the whole, Aix is most delightfully situated, and the environs are beyond conception rural and beautiful. They are a succession of vineyards relieved by groves, meadows and fields. I did not leave them without regret. The carriage drove slowly, but even under these circumstances we repeatedly stopt it.

We reached Marseilles without further occurrence; and as a ship was ready there, after two or three days spent in the company of my friends, who very kindly refused to leave me, I took my departure, and left a kingdom which I have since never ceased to think.

THE END.

Printed in Great Britain
by Amazon